Cambridge Elements

Elements in Politics and Society in Southeast Asia
edited by
Edward Aspinall
Australian National University
Meredith L. Weiss
University at Albany, SUNY

SUSTAINABLE DEVELOPMENT AND THE ENVIRONMENT IN SOUTHEAST ASIA

Pamela D. McElwee
Rutgers University

Shaftesbury Road, Cambridge CB2 8EA, United Kingdom

One Liberty Plaza, 20th Floor, New York, NY 10006, USA

477 Williamstown Road, Port Melbourne, VIC 3207, Australia

314–321, 3rd Floor, Plot 3, Splendor Forum, Jasola District Centre, New Delhi – 110025, India

103 Penang Road, #05–06/07, Visioncrest Commercial, Singapore 238467

Cambridge University Press is part of Cambridge University Press & Assessment, a department of the University of Cambridge.

We share the University's mission to contribute to society through the pursuit of education, learning and research at the highest international levels of excellence.

www.cambridge.org
Information on this title: www.cambridge.org/9781009566049

DOI: 10.1017/9781108855334

© Pamela D. McElwee 2025

This publication is in copyright. Subject to statutory exception and to the provisions of relevant collective licensing agreements, no reproduction of any part may take place without the written permission of Cambridge University Press & Assessment.

When citing this work, please include a reference to the DOI 10.1017/9781108855334

First published 2025

A catalogue record for this publication is available from the British Library

ISBN 978-1-009-56604-9 Hardback
ISBN 978-1-108-72053-3 Paperback
ISSN 2515-2998 (online)
ISSN 2515-298X (print)

Cambridge University Press & Assessment has no responsibility for the persistence or accuracy of URLs for external or third-party internet websites referred to in this publication and does not guarantee that any content on such websites is, or will remain, accurate or appropriate.

For EU product safety concerns, contact us at Calle de José Abascal, 56, 1°, 28003 Madrid, Spain, or email eugpsr@cambridge.org

Sustainable Development and the Environment in Southeast Asia

Elements in Politics and Society in Southeast Asia

DOI: 10.1017/9781108855334
First published online: July 2025

Pamela D. McElwee
Rutgers University

Author for correspondence: Pamela D. McElwee, pamela.mcelwee@rutgers.edu

Abstract: The rapid economic development experienced by Southeast Asia has come at the cost of considerable environmental degradation, including deforestation and land degradation, biodiversity loss, water and ocean pollution, rising greenhouse gas emissions, and increasing vulnerability to climate change. While sustainable development as a concept recognizes the fundamental importance of nature to future human well-being, the Sustainable Development Goals (SDGs) as a set of policies falls far short of this ideal. The SDGs, particularly the environmental goals relating to life on land, life under water, and climate action, are essentially impossible to meet in Southeast Asia, as no country is on a sustainability trajectory, but these goals are modest at best anyway. Alternative approaches that recognize trade-offs and seek to integrate across solutions, that create spaces for inclusion, and that center equity and justice could help meet SDG goals, but face considerable challenges in implementation across Southeast Asia.

Keywords: sustainable development, biodiversity, climate change, deforestation, marine pollution

© Pamela D. McElwee 2025

ISBNs: 9781009566049 (HB), 9781108720533 (PB), 9781108855334 (OC)
ISSNs: 2515-2998 (online), 2515-298X (print)

Contents

1 Southeast Asia and Sustainable Development   1

2 Sustainable Development and the SDGs   10

3 Life on Land: Challenges for Forests, Freshwater, and Biodiversity   17

4 Life Below Water: Marine and Coastal Ecosystems   32

5 Climate Action: Adaptation and Mitigation in a Changing Climate   48

6 Conclusions: The Future of Sustainable Development in Southeast Asia   60

    References   66

1 Southeast Asia and Sustainable Development

1.1 Introduction

Balancing economic growth and improving well-being while simultaneously conserving and stewarding the environment has been a key challenge for the past half-century since "sustainable development" was first introduced as a term. Since then, the concept has evolved from buzzword among environmental advocates into a global organizing framework in the form of the UN Sustainable Development Goals (SDGs), adopted by member states in 2015. Structured around seventeen key targets, the SDGs seek to align protection of the environment with improved living standards through reduced poverty and increased health and well-being, alongside economic growth, sustainable production and consumption, and peace and justice (Box 1). The SDGs have also been supplemented with other multilateral actions, including the Paris Agreement for climate in 2015 and the Kunming-Montreal Global Biodiversity Framework (GBF) adopted in 2022. Together, these goals posit that countries can and should be able to protect natural resources, tackle climate change, and provide safe and adequate levels of well-being simultaneously. Yet whether or not they will be able to do so remains a considerable question mark.

Southeast Asia is an ideal place to examine the many challenges facing countries as they attempt to address the environmental problems that have resulted from traditional economic development paths. The region encompasses a wide range of levels of development, from high-income urban Singapore to fast-growing middle classes in Malaysia, Thailand, Indonesia, and Vietnam to countries that remain stuck in low-income status like Timor-Leste, Cambodia, Laos, and Myanmar. The Southeast Asian region has experienced some of the highest economic growth rates in the world as well as the highest rates of dependency on global trade in natural resources (Gellert 2020). Relatedly, environmental degradation has been acute: Southeast Asia has the dubious distinction of having the highest rates of deforestation, the highest rates of agricultural phosphorus use, and the highest number of premature deaths from air pollution globally (Koplitz et al. 2017; MacDonald et al. 2011; Zeng et al. 2018). If anywhere in the world needs sustainable development, it is Southeast Asia.

This Element examines the environmental challenges facing the region and asks if the SDGs are a tool or a hindrance. The environmental SDGs in particular have received attention as not just important on their own, but as fundamental for achievement of the other social and economic SDGs (Blicharska et al. 2019). If the ecosystems that provide water and air alongside timber and food production are unraveled by climate change, overexploitation, pollution, and other causes, it is not just nature and biodiversity that is at risk, but human well-being (UNDP 2020).

> **Box 1 The Sustainable Development Goals**
>
> Goal 1: End poverty in all its forms everywhere
>
> Goal 2: End hunger, achieve food security and improved nutrition, and promote sustainable agriculture
>
> Goal 3: Ensure healthy lives and promote well-being for all at all ages
>
> Goal 4: Ensure inclusive and equitable quality education and promote lifelong learning opportunities for all
>
> Goal 5: Achieve gender equality and empower all women and girls
>
> Goal 6: Ensure availability and sustainable management of water and sanitation for all
>
> Goal 7: Ensure access to affordable, reliable, sustainable, and modern energy for all
>
> Goal 8: Promote sustained, inclusive, and sustainable economic growth, full and productive employment, and decent work for all
>
> Goal 9: Build resilient infrastructure, promote inclusive and sustainable industrialization, and foster innovation
>
> Goal 10: Reduce inequality within and among countries
>
> Goal 11: Make cities and human settlements inclusive, safe, resilient, and sustainable
>
> Goal 12: Ensure sustainable consumption and production patterns
>
> Goal 13: Take urgent action to combat climate change and its impacts
>
> Goal 14: Conserve and sustainably use the oceans, seas, and marine resources for sustainable development
>
> Goal 15: Protect, restore, and promote sustainable use of terrestrial ecosystems, sustainably manage forests, combat desertification, and halt and reverse land degradation and halt biodiversity loss
>
> Goal 16: Promote peaceful and inclusive societies for sustainable development, provide access to justice for all, and build effective, accountable, and inclusive institutions at all levels
>
> Goal 17: Strengthen the means of implementation and revitalize the Global Partnership for Sustainable Development

Failing to meet environmental goals thus also threatens other social targets, like reduced poverty or improved health (Figure 1).

In examining how Southeast Asian countries have approached the SDGs and sustainable development generally, several key themes emerge that are the focus of the rest of this Element. First is the interconnected nature of economic and environmental problems. Governments in Southeast Asia are not yet making the connections that economic progress, reductions in poverty, or improvements in

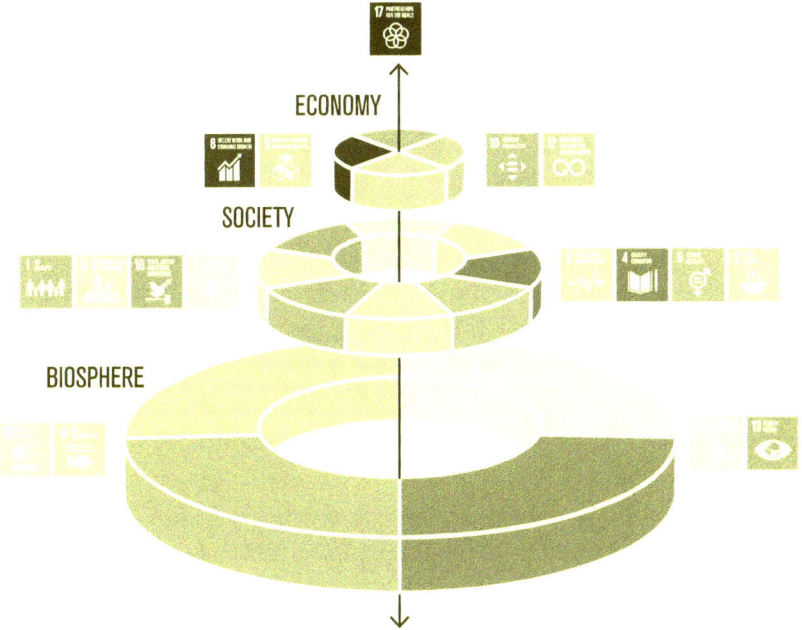

Figure 1 The environmental SDGs as a basis for all SDGs
Source: Azote for Stockholm Resilience Centre, Stockholm University CC BY-ND 3.0.

health could be at risk from not addressing environmental degradation, but rather the opposite has occurred: Concerns that growth might be slowed if aggressive environmental action is taken have dominated. Second, interconnections among the SDGs emphasize the need for cross-actor and cross-scale collaborations. In an ideal world, the SDGs could help to bring together new coalitions and to prioritize new ways of doing development. Yet the limited political and economic space in many Southeast Asian countries has prevented new collaborative policies and actions and stifled creative solutions.

Finally, there has been a lack of attention to justice in pursuit of the SDGs, both in Southeast Asia and elsewhere. The costs of economic and environmental change have often been borne by the marginalized while elites stand to benefit, or rural people have made sacrifices while urban dwellers accrue advantages. Some of the most encouraging potential solutions come from the emergence of rural–urban political coalitions or by recognizing the rights of Indigenous peoples to territories and thus foregrounding marginalized peoples' interests. But while attention to justice and rights-based approaches are emerging, concrete results and reframing of sustainable development pathways remain stubbornly elusive. At the more than halfway point to 2030, hoped-for promises of inclusive, integrated, and sustainable development are at risk (Filho et al. 2023).

1.2 Southeast Asia as SDG Test Bed

The economy of the Association of Southeast Asian Nations (ASEAN) region has doubled over the past fifteen years, from US$2.02 trillion in 2009 to US$4.08 trillion in 2024.[1] If the region were a single country, it would be the fifth largest economy in the world after the United States, China, Japan, and Germany. Southeast Asia is often presented as a success story for poverty reduction, dropping from 45 percent of the total population in 1990 to approximately 15 percent by 2017 (ASEAN 2017). However, this economic success has come at considerable cost to the environment, particularly as many countries achieved economic growth primarily from natural resource expropriation. Wetlands, peatlands, and forests have been converted to globally exported agricultural commodities like palm oil, rice, and rubber or sawn into timber and woodchips; mountains and coasts have been stripped for minerals, coal, and sand; and oceans, rivers, and lakes have been trawled for fish or drained for development (Gellert 2020; Pas-ong and Lebel 2000; Simpson 2018). As Gellert (2020) notes, "Rather than unfortunate or ill-managed externalities of otherwise successful development, degradation has been inherent in Southeast Asia's mode of capitalist development" (p. 373). While export-oriented economic choices and subsequent environmental degradation have been experienced globally, as a region Southeast Asia stands out. Nearly 90 percent of aquaculture consumed globally is produced in Asia, as is 90 percent of rubber and palm oil (see Box 2). Industrial production has also expanded across the region for everything from electronics to textiles to steel. These industrial zones and world factories have driven labor migration and urban expansion, while simultaneously increasing land conflicts, water and air pollution, and greenhouse gas (GHG) emissions (Rigg 2020; Savage 2006).

Faced with these myriad challenges, Southeast Asian nations have embraced the general concept embedded within the SDGs of sustainable development for all. Every country has signed on to the SDGs, and many have issued individual country reports on how they are progressing (ASEAN 2017). There have also been national processes to adopt and "localize" the SDGs; for example, Laos has declared a Goal 18 called "Lives safe from unexploded ordnance," while other countries have included their own philosophies of development. The Philippines stresses a "life that is strongly rooted in family and community, comfortable, and secure," while Thailand promotes a "Sufficiency Economy Philosophy as our homegrown approach that focuses on human empowerment, resilience, and environmental conservation." While some countries like

---

[1] Based on trend data collected by the International Monetary Fund: www.imf.org/external/data mapper/NGDPD@WEO/SEQ.

Box 2 THE SUSTAINABILITY CHALLENGES OF PALM OIL

Approximately 90 percent of the global oil palm area and 85 percent of production is in Southeast Asia. The plant itself (*Elaeis guineensis*) is native to West Africa, and plantations were first introduced to the region by the Dutch and British during the colonial era. Palm oil is in high demand globally for its use in a range of products, from cosmetics to processed food to biofuels. Oil palm trees can be grown in poor soils and planting has driven the conversion of tropical forests and draining of peat swamps, often by fire, despite the fact that laws on the books call for planting on degraded land only. Oil palm expansion is currently the number one driver of forest loss: From 2001 to 2016, Indonesia, Malaysia, and Papua New Guinea lost around thirty-one million hectares (Mha) of forest, strongly correlated to where oil palm concessions were granted (Gatti et al. 2018). These peatlands are rich storehouses of carbon, and some estimates have concluded that nearly 10 percent of global carbon emissions have been a result of Indonesia's oil palm-driven forest conversion (Carlson et al. 2012). Draining peat soils also diminishes ecosystem services like water regulation and habitat for biodiversity, particularly for orangutans (Dislich et al. 2017). Of over 405 protected areas (PAs) designated in Indonesia and Malaysia, 395 have been encroached upon by palm oil plantations (Xu et al. 2022) (Figure 2)

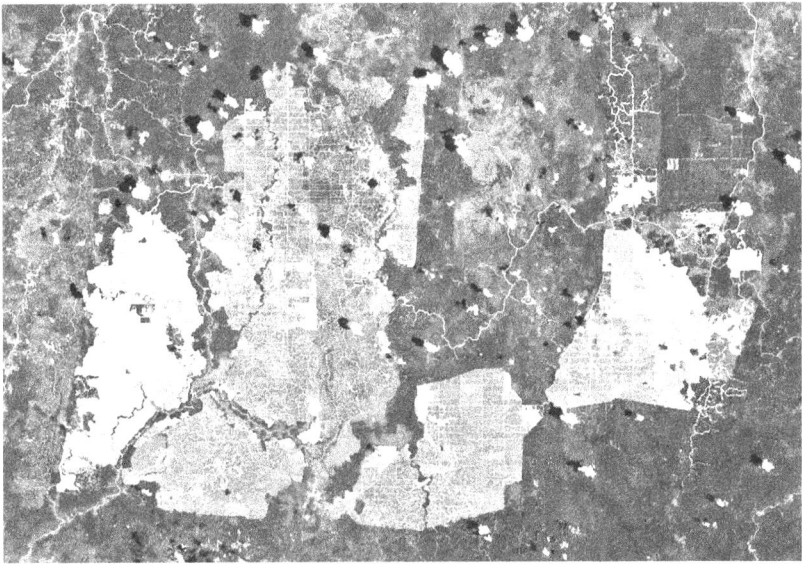

Figure 2 Oil palm expansion in Indonesian Borneo

Box 2 (cont.)

Land use changes show newly deforested patches and existing palm oil plantations, as seen by the European Space Agency's (ESA) Copernicus Sentinel-2 satellite in February 2019. Source: ESA, CC BY-SA 3.0 IGO.

When peat soils burn, the process generates significant air pollution and haze, raising mortality risks and costing billions in economic damages. Up to 90 percent of transboundary haze in insular Southeast Asia is linked to peat fires from commercial palm oil plantations in Indonesia and Malaysia. An extremely severe 1997–1998 event led to economic costs to Singapore of US$163–286 million and to Indonesia of between US$9 and 20 billion (Islam et al. 2016). The health risks of haze events include increased risks of hospitalization, respiratory infections, asthma, cancers, and excess deaths. For a 2015 haze event set off by fires in Kalimantan and Sumatra, excess deaths were estimated to be 91,600 in Indonesia, 6,500 in Malaysia, and 2,200 in Singapore (Koplitz et al. 2016).

Approximately two-thirds of Indonesia's palm oil estate are large industrial plantations, while one-third are smallholders with less than 25 hectares (Gaveau et al. 2017). Oil palm expansion has been driven by land acquisition by plantations, alongside producer incentives for households, leaving many smallholders voluntarily involved but precariously benefiting (Habibi 2023). Smallholders often contract with mill operators for technical support in planting and processing, binding them to unfair commodity chains dominated by elites, with highly complex supply chains linking growers, processors, and large agrobusinesses. Unilever, the world's largest buyer of palm oil, and other transnational companies strongly control the terms of trade (Brandi et al. 2015). There have been numerous accusations of false promises to smallholders by plantation developers, including labor abuses and expropriation of Indigenous peoples from their lands (Colchester and Chao 2011). While some farmers have seen livelihood benefits, other dispossessions have split communities (Li and Semedi 2021; Santika et al. 2021).

Concerns about the environmental costs have led to calls for consumer boycotts of palm oil. In response, Indonesia has a moratorium on new concessions in primary forests, although enforcement has suffered (Austin et al. 2017). The Roundtable on Sustainable Palm Oil, founded in 2004, is a voluntary market scheme that links buyers and producers to encourage reduced deforestation in return for certification as

Box 2 (cont.)

"sustainable" and higher price premiums. New plantations must not clear existing forest and must fulfill a number of other steps, such as protection of sensitive habitats. However, only around 20 percent of palm oil production is certified, and the costs to get certified tend to be expensive, which makes it difficult for smallholders to participate (Brandi et al. 2015; Ruysschaert and Salles 2014). Certification has had some effects on reducing deforestation, but mainly because most certified plantations are older ones with less natural forest remaining anyway (Carlson et al. 2018). At the farm level, certified farms do not appear to be more sustainable than noncertified across environmental, social, or economic measures (Morgans et al. 2018).

In more dramatic measures, the EU has passed an EU Deforestation Regulation to stop the import of any product linked to deforestation, which would include all noncertified palm oil, and is also moving to phase out biofuels by 2030. Malaysia and Indonesia have strongly objected to the World Trade Organization about these measures, seeing them as an unfair trade barrier (Warren-Thomas et al. 2023), and litigation over these measures has already started.

ASEAN has brokered several agreements to tackle transboundary haze pollution, including a Haze-free Roadmap 2023–2030 and a Peatland Management Strategy, although these have largely failed to address root causes of the problem given ASEAN's tendency toward "non-interference" (Zhang and Savage 2019). Citizens have begun monitoring air pollution themselves, with smartphone apps used to measure particulate levels and to share readings on social media, alongside the emergence of civil society organizations like the People's Movement to Stop Haze in Singapore (Varkkey 2022). Yet the problem will continue to get worse as climate change creates drought and wind conditions that exacerbate fires and spread them further afield. Further, critiques of the problem in the media have tended to be muted, given limited political space in Malaysia and Singapore in particular (Forsyth 2014), and these criticisms have not usually focused on the justice aspects of the problem, such as unequal benefits from plantation development and elite capture of political decision-making (Hasfi et al. 2021).

Vietnam have merely mapped some selected SDGs onto existing national development targets to be dealt with by ministries and agencies, with little civil society input (Vu and Long 2023), other national SDG planning processes were more participatory (Cheng et al. 2021).

However, despite the initial interest and localized adoption, an examination of where countries are in achieving the SDGs reveals fractures and even stagnation. On some targets, like quality education (SDG 4), improvements in the region are impressive. For others, particularly the environmental goals, there is little evidence of any progress at all, with rates of deforestation, water overuse, biodiversity loss, air pollution, and GHG emissions continuing to rise.[2] The complex interactions between economic decisions and environmental outcomes that account for this lack of progress can be seen in Voluntary National Reviews (VNR), regular report cards issued on how countries are meeting the SDGs.[3] Rather than seeing the environmental SDGs as critical for realization of the other goals, governments have tended to view them as separate, siloed, and easily ignored. On SDG 13 on climate action, only Singapore, Cambodia, and Myanmar are getting closer to targets (which are themselves fairly unambitious). On SDG 14 on ocean and coastal management, only Malaysia and the Philippines are making limited progress (namely around extending marine protected areas [MPAs]). On SDG 15 on life on land, every single Southeast Asian country is either stagnating or declining in terms of meeting targets for protecting and restoring forests, water, and species (Sachs et al. 2023). As an example of these trade-offs, Box 2 discusses palm oil as a "wicked" sustainability problem and the inadequacies of current solutions.[4] Like palm oil, many other sustainability challenges in Southeast Asia defy easy solutions and will be politically difficult.

1.3 Organization of the Element

In this Element, I discuss current environmental challenges across both mainland and insular Southeast Asia, starting with a brief discussion of the larger global context of sustainable development (Section 2). I then turn to individual SDGs to examine the present situation, proposed pathways, and alternative actions that could provide a different perspective. Section 3 discusses *SDG 15: Life on Land*, dealing with forests, freshwater, and biodiversity. Section 4 addresses *SDG 14: Life Below Water* on marine and coastal issues, such as ocean pollution and overfishing. Section 5 covers *SDG 13: Climate Action* including GHG emissions, hazard vulnerability, and adaptation to climate change. While other SDGs, such

---

[2] In general, Southeast Asia is generally in the middle of the pack on the SDGs, with better progress than Sub-Saharan Africa, but below East Asia, North America, and Europe.

[3] Most Southeast Asian countries have filed at least one Voluntary National Review report in either 2021 or 2023, with only Laos and Myanmar not providing an update. These reports are available at: https://sustainabledevelopment.un.org/vnrs/

[4] Wicked problems are those that are complex, often symptoms of related problems, and without clearly defined solutions. See Lönngren and Poeck (2021).

as water (SDG 6) or energy use (SDG 7), also are related to these sectors, for the sake of space, they are not addressed directly.

Throughout the Element, I primarily take a political ecology approach, which challenges scholars to dig deeper into how terms like "underdevelopment" or "vulnerability" get adopted in the first place, as well as what they mean and to whom (Taylor 2013). Political ecology approaches also aim to increase understanding of the multi-scalar drivers of change and concentric circles of power that characterize resource control, access, and resistance (Bryant 1998). Each section examines the key drivers of environmental decline, noting that they often originate from outside the region, via trade connections or external investments. However, these drivers are not directly addressed in most Southeast Asian country plans and policies to meet SDG targets, which instead often focus on surface outcomes (e.g., increasing percentages of PAs) rather than addressing deeper causes (e.g., asking why lands were degraded in the first place).

Additionally, failures to achieve sustainable development are not for lack of policies: ASEAN countries in their VNRs identify large numbers of actions (Elder and Ellis 2023). But all too often, these reflect traditional conceptions of market-friendly policies and export-led economic development, or siloed and piecemeal approaches that fail to address the underlying root causes. Despite country-level differences, common patterns do emerge, including problems of elite capture and corruption, unclear agency for who should and can act, and shrinking space for political advocacy by civil society to chart alternative visions. Each section thus also looks carefully at who profits from failures to achieve sustainability, whether it is individual corporations, wealthier farmers, or richer countries thriving at the expense of poorer ones.

However, alternative visions of what sustainable development might look like do exist, often driven from the bottom-up by civil society actors, marginalized peoples, and their transnational partners. Citizens have joined together across rural–urban divides to protest marine pollution in Vietnam and coal mining in the Philippines. Community-based natural resource management across lands and seas has succeeded in providing sustainable livelihoods for smallholder production through collective action. Adaptive and resilient pathways to address climate change that are grounded in values of equity have taken hold, in sites from small pockets of coastal Indonesia to urban Singapore. Creative development projects that innovate across food, water, and health have helped bring attention to the need to tackle interlinked and complex challenges, while contributing to increased resilience against climate change. These examples and more are noted in the sections to follow.

Yet these kinds of integrated, collaborative, and justice-oriented initiatives are also seen as a threat by some of the undemocratic and increasingly authoritarian governments in the region. Many countries have low citizen participation in environmental policymaking and weak rule of law, alongside high levels of corruption and rising inequity. Multiple military coups (Thailand and Myanmar), single-party rule (Vietnam, Laos, Cambodia, Singapore), and backsliding toward authoritarianism (Philippines, Indonesia) can make it difficult to envision different positive futures (McGregor et al. 2018; Teehankee 2019). Siloed ministries, low technological capacity, and weak regional cooperation also create barriers (Varkkey 2018). As a regional coordination organization, ASEAN has produced many reports on environment and sustainability, but not much cooperative action (Elliott 2012; Simpson 2018). The uncertain role that China will play in driving unsustainability in the region also looms large. Overcoming these myriad obstacles will be a major task for any alternative visions of sustainability governance in Southeast Asia.

2 Sustainable Development and the SDGs

2.1 Introduction: A Brief History of Sustainable Development

There has long been a debate on whether economic growth is compatible with environmental protection or whether there should be limits to resource consumption. Rising evidence of environmental destruction in the 1960s coincided with pictures of Earth taken from the first lunar landing, showing the beauty and interconnectedness of the globe. The idea that there are finite resources on this fragile blue planet were expanded by the publication of *The Limits to Growth* in 1972, which presented various scenarios of harsh future choices given unrestrained economic growth and concomitant environmental degradation. The first multilateral environmental conference was held that same year: the United Nations Conference on the Human Environment in Stockholm. Over 113 countries sent representatives to discuss the declaration that "The protection and improvement of the human environment is a major issue that affects the well-being of people and economic development throughout the world."

The conference concluded with no major advances, although the United Nations Environment Programme (UNEP) was founded and charged with combining the South's concern over poverty issues with Northern countries' environmental interests (Ivanova 2010). The UNEP later collaborated with the International Union of the Conservation of Nature and the World Wildlife Fund to draft the World Conservation Strategy (WCS) in 1980, and it is this report that the Oxford English Dictionary lists as including the first widespread use of the concept of "sustainable development" (Vira 2015). The WCS was followed by the creation of the World Commission on Environment and Development in 1983, chaired by Prime Minister Gro Harlem Brundtland of Norway. Their definition is still the most commonly used one today: "development that meets the needs of the present without compromising the ability of future generations to meet their own needs."

At the 1992 UN Rio "Earth Summit," symbolically held on the twentieth anniversary of the Stockholm conference, countries presented a five-year stocktake on achieving the goals of the Brundtland commission. One of the documents adopted, Agenda 21, outlined steps that countries could take to address both economic development and environmental improvements, such as attention to human health affected by both poverty and pollution, the need for integrating responses across air, water, land, and seas, and the safe development of new technologies to improve human flourishing. The adoption of the UN Millennium Development Goals (MDGs) in 2000 signaled a shift from summits to formal target setting. Seen primarily as a guide for poorer countries, the MDGs led to some successes, notably in improving access to water and sanitation as well as reducing extreme poverty. However, Target 7 on achieving "environmental sustainability" was an abject failure (Liverman 2018). Criticisms of the MDGs spurred a new process to replace them and ensure that they would apply equally to the global North and to better integrate the environment and well-being goals (Fukuda-Parr 2016). A High-Level Panel on a post-2015 development agenda, cochaired by Indonesia's then-President Susilo Bambang Yudhoyono, reported recommendations that ultimately became the SDGs, adopted in September 2015.

2.2 From Buzzwords to Policy Targets

When the SDGs were first announced, there were mixed reviews. Some praised the large variety of topics addressed and their global scope, while others considered them a laundry list that was a "mess" and "confused" (Carr 2015; Sultana 2018). Critical scholars have particularly argued that the SDGs promote market-oriented governance to produce entrepreneurial subjects, rather than focusing on widespread and more just outcomes. This is seen in the "focus on public–private partnerships, quantitative outcome measures, solutions through markets, and individual rather than collective strategies" (Liverman 2018). While proponents laud such steps as ways to increase efficiency and responsiveness of governance, others have expressed concern that prior experience with neoliberal policies has often resulted in loss of access to natural resources, particularly for poorer peoples (Büscher et al. 2012).

Countries are supposed to integrate the SDGs into national policies and road maps, although implementation is not legally binding. The SDGs provide only broad targets, do not explicitly address who has agency and should take action, and do not identify specific policies that are most likely to lead to success. For example, the climate action goal has no targets related to reducing GHG emissions, the one action that is universally recognized as necessary to reduce global temperatures (IPCC 2022). So far there is little evidence that the SDGs have instigated major policy changes, whether in terms of increasing financial resources or pushing signatories toward more coherent and integrated policies (Biermann et al. 2022). As there are so many targets, some countries have focused selectively on those considered to align with their preexisting development priorities, such as economic growth and poverty reduction rather than the full suite of SDGs (Forestier and Kim 2020). For example, despite attention to the SDGs' being integrative – all for one and one for all – in reality, not all goals are synergistic. Having individual targets for land, oceans, and climate (not to mention energy, water, and other sectors) replicates long-standing siloed objectives for natural resources management (Tosun and Leininger 2017). Some countries have simply ignored the environmental goals and focused on economic ones, not seeing the environmental goals as fundamental to well-being, but rather distractions from it.

Other countries simply do not have sufficient resources to try to achieve all seventeen SDGs and so they have fixed on only some as most relevant (Fukuda-Parr 2016). For example, Timor-Leste's 2023 VNR only addresses the health and well-being goals, while Cambodia prioritizes SDG 6 (water and sanitation), SDG 7 (energy), SDG 9 (industry), SDG 11 (cities), and SDG 17 (partnerships). Indonesia's most recent VNR shows a focus on a more limited set of goals and targets centered around industry, health, and social protection, rather than the full suite of SDGs, while Vietnam's VNR mostly ignores climate mitigation.

2.3 Theories of Change for the SDGs

One of the biggest challenges to adopting policies to achieve the SDGs is their failure to identify the drivers of negative trends and pinpoint who is to blame (Lim et al. 2018). For example, what has driven the declines in global forest cover in recent years? The SDG goals and targets simply state the need to reduce deforestation and increase reforestation, but do not specify what the drivers of negative trends are, which makes it difficult to know how to tackle them (Eisenmenger et al. 2020). These key drivers have been identified elsewhere as economic growth, excess consumption, global trade, population change and urbanization, conflict, and values and behavioral choices, among others (Ebi et al. 2020; IPBES 2019). These drivers in turn are rooted in long-standing global systems of political economy that reflect historical power and economic relations, as world systems theory and concepts of ecologically unequal exchange have long posited (Hornborg 1998; Srinivasan et al. 2008). But it is difficult for countries to plan for sustainable development if these historical and structural roots of poverty, hunger, or environmental destruction are not explicitly acknowledged (Sexsmith and McMichael 2015).

This lack of a theory of change for the SDGs has led to countries placing too much hope in economic growth, which is and always has been a key driver of environmental degradation. Such a position is embedded in SDG 8, which calls for promoting "sustained, inclusive and sustainable economic growth," and which sets up an explicit conflict with the environmental SDGs (Hickel 2019; Pradhan et al. 2017). This optimism that economic growth is compatible with environmental protection bears a strong influence of modernization theory, which argues poverty can be overcome with economic expansion. According to this theory, while environmental degradation and pollution may be part of the growth curve at the beginning, eventually, pollution will be reduced as countries become wealthier. This has essentially been the outcome Southeast Asian countries were hoping for in their economic development choices: grow now, and clean up later.

In reality, numerous environmental impacts *increase* linearly as incomes rise, rather than declining over time, particularly GHG emissions and overall resource consumption. This relationship between quality of life and environmental impact, often measured as an ecological "footprint," can be seen visually in Figure 3.

Figure 3 Relationships between national well-being and environmental impact
Source: Adapted from www.sustainabledevelopmentindex.org/.

Countries that have a high quality of life, as measured by indicators of income, health, and education like the Human Development Index (HDI), also have larger environmental footprints as measured by resource consumption and pollution (Wackernagel et al. 2017). Some countries do show higher quality of life with more modest environmental costs, a glass-half full reading; however, only one country (Sri Lanka) occupies the key intersection of relatively high human development and low resource use. The SDGs are predicated on countries being able to occupy this space, and yet only one country actually does.

The Southeast Asian situation highlights this conundrum: Nations like Singapore have attained a higher economic status through greater impacts on the environment and high resource use, while lower consumption nations like Laos have done a better job of living within their environmental means, but at costs to their HDI. Growing consumption levels mean several ASEAN countries are now above the global average of "ecological footprints," including Singapore, Brunei, and Malaysia (Iha et al. 2015). A recent new approach to the HDI has tried to "adjust" well-being rankings by subtracting planetary (e.g., environmental) impacts from them; this brings many so-called highly developed nations downward if their development achievements have come at the cost of high consumption or the offshoring of degrading activities elsewhere. Brunei, for example, drops dramatically from a high HDI to a much lower planetary-adjusted HDI because of the country's high consumption and export of petroleum (UNDP 2020). Under a planetary-adjusted HDI, the highest ranking Southeast Asian country is Thailand at #43, with Vietnam at #55, Singapore at #64, Indonesia at #75, and Malaysia at #78.

Yet despite the considerable evidence to the contrary, many country development plans continue to assert that growth, development and the environment are fully compatible, and trade-offs can be managed. For most Southeast Asian countries, a "green neoliberal" development model has assumed that prosperity can be built from global commodities exported to the rest of world (Gellert 2020; Goldman 2001), which requires more infrastructure, land regularization, and capital. This faith in the market is common across both long-standing open economies like Singapore as well as post-socialist ones like Vietnam. Another prominent recent concept has been the promise of "green growth": expanding an economy while resource use or pollution declines (also known as decoupling). For many Southeast Asian countries, green growth has become a key organizing principle for them to optimistically meet the SDGs through continuing their existing pathways of economic development (ADB & UNU 2017; OECD 2016). A recent ASEAN report has proposed a goal of increasing private-sector investment in sustainability tenfold to generate US$3 trillion in green business by 2030 (ASEAN 2021). But there is little empirical evidence to suggest that this scale is feasible, or that economic growth can be achieved without exceeding planetary boundaries (Hickel 2018, 2019; Randers et al. 2019). While decoupling of CO_2 emissions and GDP has occurred in a few European countries and the United Kingdom, decoupling of other forms of resource consumption have proven much more difficult, particularly in Southeast Asia (Hickel and Kallis 2019).

2.4 Reframing the SDGs

What if there are other ways to define good environmental governance and high quality of life other than the SDGs' concepts of continued economic growth and traditional development pathways? In contrast to the business-as-usual approaches seen in Southeast Asia, other concepts and actions for addressing sustainable development have been proposed, including "(i) cultivating collective action by creating inclusive decision spaces for stakeholder interaction across multiple sectors and scales; (ii) making difficult trade-offs, focusing on equity, justice and fairness; and (iii) ensuring mechanisms exist to hold societal actors to account regarding decision-making, investment, action, and outcomes" (Bowen et al. 2017). Alternative visions of well-being built on strong ecological systems, alongside policy pathways that help reframe the drivers of unsustainability, can help realize these governance challenges. Such alternatives help identify key drivers of degradation and treat environmental outcomes as interconnected to well-being; extend inclusion in the design and implementation of sustainable development policies; and seek to ensure benefits for all, particularly those who have been most negatively affected by existing environmental degradation.

Reframing sustainability problems as interconnected can improve the management of trade-offs and enhance potential synergies as well as expand the definitions of who benefits from interventions (Liu et al. 2018). The SDG's sectoral targets have been contrasted with "nexus" approaches that integrate across systems to find multifunctional interventions, recognizing that complex and wicked problems require more integrated solutions, such as managing water–energy–food systems together. These integrated approaches also acknowledge that environmental problems and human societies are embedded in linked socio-ecological systems, not external to them (Norström et al. 2014). Integrated SDG implementation would focus attention to interlinkages across sectors (e.g., horizontal links across environmental goals as well as to finance and economics, agriculture, energy, transportation, and others) (Liu et al. 2018); across scales of governance (e.g., vertical links from central states to local villages and vice versa) (Breuer et al. 2023); and the interdependencies between low-, medium-, and high-income countries (Stafford-Smith et al. 2017).

Better understanding of the interconnected nature of drivers and problems also highlights the uneven benefits countries have received from resource overexploitation and unsustainability to date (Leach et al. 2018). The neoliberal and market-based governance that has dominated many SDG plans can be contrasted with "rights-based approaches," in which human rights and equity drive policy goals, rather than the market (Arts 2017). Rights-based approaches assert that states are duty-bearers – for example, depending on legal regimes, they may have a duty to ensure clean environments or good health – and if they fail, there should be remedies for justice by those who have been underserved. Expanding rights-based approaches allow claims to be advanced by even the marginalized, creating accountability for other actors, and foregrounding values of equity, transparency, and empowerment (Ensor et al. 2015).

Such an approach is in theory possible within Southeast Asia, given that the ASEAN charter includes a statement that "Every person has the right to an adequate standard of living ... including ... the right to a safe, clean and sustainable environment." However, in reality, environmental justice has often fallen short, with a number of policies actually increasing vulnerability or failing to enforce rights to basic needs, as later sections will show. Where there are rights-based approaches in place in Southeast Asia, wider groups have benefitted, including from community forestry, decentralized fisheries comanagement, Indigenous and community conserved areas (ICCAs), and locally led climate adaptation. These rights-based approaches and entitlements can make clear who has profited off degradation (in many cases, corporations and the wealthy) and who has not (Indigenous peoples, urban slum dwellers or the land-dispossessed). Yet there is also outright hostility to rights-based approaches and ideas in some countries, particularly the post-socialist, single-party governed countries that see human rights discourse as a political threat (Vu and Long 2023).

Reframing sustainable development to provide more just outcomes also requires social inclusion and participation. Inclusion can help identify and focus attention on those currently left behind, as well as expand opportunities and decision-making to more actors and more voices. In principle this is possible: All the VNRs that Southeast Asian countries have submitted (Myanmar and Laos have not) mention the importance of civil society in helping achieve SDGs. In reality, SDG planning and participation is often at the surface-level, and there remain numerous structural barriers to realization of environmental rights. For example, in most ASEAN countries there is a lack of recognition for many Indigenous communities and limited legal mechanisms for substantive or procedural rights (Gellers and Jeffords 2019; Masud et al. 2018).

These elements of interconnection, inclusion, and justice work together. For example, where closed political systems limit the amount of space for civil society, there is less opportunity to advocate for more equitable and integrated solutions (Gritten et al. 2019).

The following three sections look specifically at the SDG goals for land, oceans, and climate, examining how they have been interpreted in policy adoption and change in Southeast Asia, alongside analysis of current inadequacies. Each section also highlights other visions and concepts of sustainability that have emerged and which engage with concepts of interconnection, inclusion, and justice, or which identify economic growth as a negative driver and propose alternative solutions.

3 Life on Land: Challenges for Forests, Freshwater, and Biodiversity

3.1 Introduction

Southeast Asia is home to 15 percent of the world's tropical forests, alongside some of the richest freshwater ecosystems, supporting the livelihoods of hundreds of millions and serving as storehouses of biodiversity and important sources of clean water, soil fertility, and carbon sequestration (Estoque et al. 2019). However, the region is also a global hot spot for forest, wetland, and biodiversity loss: From 2001 to 2015, 39 Mha of forests were converted to other uses (Curtis et al. 2018), and a booming illegal wildlife trade worth billions of dollars increases threats to species (Lee et al. 2014). These impacts have been driven by economic development demands, poor governance, corruption, and other drivers.

SDG 15 addresses "life on land" through an overarching goal to "Protect, restore and promote sustainable use of terrestrial ecosystems, sustainably manage forests, combat desertification, and halt and reverse land degradation and halt biodiversity loss." Yet the SDG targets have little to say about what the drivers of forest and biodiversity declines are and how to combat them. Because these underlying drivers are often linked to faraway consumers, generating solutions that can address these globally telecoupled[5] ties has been difficult. General approaches to ecosystem conservation, like expansion of PAs, has been the primary policy adopted in Southeast Asia, but these zones do little to stem the tide of demand for land, particularly the rise of economic drivers of land grabbing that have emerged in the past decades. Other approaches, like biodiversity corridors, may even serve as greenwashing to distract from the

---
[5] The term "telecoupling" has been used to describe the impacts of environmental change in one place on another (Liu et al. 2018).

impacts of infrastructure development. Other more bottom-up responses that foreground rights and justice, like ICCAs, are emerging, but only on small scales in a few countries. In general, equity-focused and collaborative solutions remain stubbornly small-scale.

3.2 Drivers of Change

Approximately one-third of Southeast Asia's forest cover is found on the mainland, and two-thirds in insular areas: The total forest cover was around 268 Mha in 1990, dropping to 236 Mha by 2010, an annual loss of 1.75–2.4 Mha (~0.67 percent per year) (Kondo et al. 2022). The negative impacts of widespread deforestation include soil erosion and land subsidence, increased risks of floods and droughts, and loss of biodiversity and increases in disease, all of which cause declines in human well-being (Hu et al. 2021; Wolff et al. 2021). Crops that have replaced forests are vulnerable to low water availability, erosion, and wind damage, all of which natural forests had previously buffered (Ahrends et al. 2015). Deforestation also results in significant carbon emissions when forests are burned, creating transboundary pollution and haze (see Box 2).

While deforestation rates have recently slowed in some countries (Malaysia, Philippines, Vietnam), for others, losses are accelerating. Indonesia, Myanmar, and Thailand accounted for around 80 percent of total forest loss in the region in the past two decades, with deforestation hot spots concentrated in Sumatra and Borneo (where nearly half of forest cover present in 2000 was lost by 2010 (Miettinen et al. 2011)) and the lower Mekong Basin and northern Myanmar (Imai et al. 2018; Mao et al. 2023). The primary cause of deforestation in the past few decades has been commodity crop expansion, accounting for an estimated 78 percent of losses, followed by forest exploitation for timber (13 percent) (Curtis et al. 2018). Notably, while Southeast Asian countries have often blamed swidden (shifting) agriculture practiced by ethnic minorities and Indigenous peoples for forest loss, in fact it is permanent conversion of forests to cash crop agriculture that is by far the biggest driver.

Insular Southeast Asia has experienced the highest level of deforestation among all global tropical regions since the 1990s. Indonesia dropped from an estimated 87 percent forest cover in 1950 to less than 50 percent today as a result of heavy logging in the 1970–1980s and accelerated expansion of oil palm starting in the 1990s (Tsujino et al. 2016). Much of this was on peatlands, wet carbon-rich swamps that are ill-suited to other forms of agriculture. More than 60 percent of the world's tropical peatlands are in Southeast Asia, but these have declined, on average 2.2 percent per year, a rate nearly twice that of other forest types. Indonesia is now the largest GHG emitter in the region (see Section 5), with land use change accounting for over half of the country's total emissions, driven largely by oil palm expansion (Austin et al. 2019; Stibig et al. 2014).

In mainland Southeast Asia, most deforestation in the past two decades has been in the forest frontiers of Myanmar and Thailand (Xiao et al. 2023), alongside newer hot spots of commodity production like Cambodia (Chen et al. 2024). For the mainland, rubber (another globally traded commodity) has been the most important driver of land use change. Southeast Asia supplies nearly three-quarters of the world's rubber, and at least 4 Mha of natural forests have been converted for production, including in key biodiversity-rich areas (Ahrends et al. 2015; Wang et al. 2023).

Narratives of "unused" or "underused" land in frontier areas have driven much of the agricultural expansion into forests: not only oil palm and rubber, but also coffee, cacao, maize, cassava, sugar, shrimp, and acacia (Hall 2011; Li 2018; Wong et al. 2022). The commodity crops produced by forest conversion are in high demand globally: Nearly 20 percent of commodities are traded within the region, while 12 percent go to China (ASEAN 2017). The rest are exported farther afield, creating telecoupled markets where consumers elsewhere essentially "offshore" impacts onto Southeast Asia (Winkler et al. 2021). The United States, for example, essentially "uses" around 5 percent of Southeast Asia's croplands through their imports, while Europe uses 11 percent and Japan 8 percent (Yu et al. 2013).

The promises of profits from agricultural commodities has also driven global capital to seek out speculative land investments, and large-scale land deals for the production of food and biofuel crops have accelerated with financial, energy, and food crises that have occurred since 2007–2008. Southeast Asia now accounts for around 20 percent of all land "grabbing" deals recorded by the Land Matrix database (likely an undercount), with the most significant hot spots in Indonesia (172 recorded deals), Cambodia (120 deals), and Laos (67 deals).[6] In Cambodia, economic concessions and development projects have resulted in investors now controlling around 36 percent of all agricultural lands (Davis et al. 2015). Some communities have tried to resist large-scale plantations when faced with dispossession, but many of their actions – protests, arson, trespass – have not halted plantation expansion (Dwyer 2022; Kenney-Lazar et al. 2018). These processes of accumulation and enclosure of highland commodity frontiers are responsible for at least 8 Mha of total forest loss (Zeng et al. 2018).

Some commodity frontiers are more smallholder-driver (albeit with strong state support), as in the case of rubber, while others are primarily plantation-driven, such as oil palm, with large agribusiness conglomerates the main owners (Kenney-Lazar

---

[6] https://landmatrix.org/, accessed August 2024.

and Ishikawa 2019). Changes to land laws over the past two decades, such as the "Turning Land into Capital" policy adopted by Lao PDR in 2006, have tended to favor large-scale investors (Kenney-Lazar et al. 2023), as did Circular 34 on "Criteria for 'poor' forest classification" in Vietnam, which facilitated the conversion of natural forests to rubber plantations (Phuc and Nghi 2014): Both cases show undercurrents of corruption influencing decision-making. In cross-country analysis, land concessions have been associated with poorer economic outcomes for smallholders and in some cases food insecurity, leading to potential for declining outcomes in meeting SDGs 1 and 2 (Appelt et al. 2022). While the cross-regional and power-asymmetric nature of land deals between finance-rich countries of the North and resource-rich countries of the South have garnered attention in recent years (Liao and Agrawal 2024), a significant proportion of the large-scale investment has occurred within Southeast Asia, as land-constrained countries (Singapore, Malaysia, Vietnam) send investments into poorer areas (Laos, Cambodia, Myanmar) (see Box 3).

Box 3 South–South land grabbing

While the increasing scale and scope of land grabbing in Southeast Asia has been laid at the foot of global neoliberalism (Schoenberger et al. 2017), the reality is more complicated. Vietnam is now the number one and number three investor in Laos and Cambodia, respectively, on par with far richer China, South Korea, and Malaysia. Legal restrictions on large-scale investments and the continued dominance of state-owned agricultural and forest enterprises in Vietnam's rural areas have created a situation where capital is "pushed out" of Vietnam to reshape environmental governance possibilities in Laos and Cambodia. This is a different model than China's "developmental outsourcing," where land acquisitions have been aimed at food and fuel production considered essential for the development of China (Hofman and Ho 2012). In Vietnam, strong state ownership and management of forest lands has resulted in more than half the forest land area being managed by different organizations associated with the state (McElwee 2016b). With this amount of land "locked up," privately held companies have fewer places available for investment in-country and have expanded elsewhere, as seen in the case of Hoanh Anh Gia Lai (HAGL).

The HAGL group is run by one of Vietnam's richest men, whose wealth arose from early investments in timber and minerals in the Central Highlands of Vietnam, built on his ties to provincial authorities who granted licenses for sawmills and furniture factories in the 1990s as Vietnam's economy opened.

Box 3 (cont.)

Since 2002, HAGL has moved to major investments in hydropower, rubber, and sugarcane in Laos and Cambodia, as well as land development and electricity in Vietnam, particularly in Ho Chi Minh City, where rumors of corrupt connections abound. HAGL was the first Vietnamese company to list global depository receipts (worth over US$ 50 million) on the London Stock Exchange in 2011 to be used for rubber plantation and hydropower projects.[7] HAGL had planned 43,500 hectares of rubber in Vietnam, Laos, and Cambodia, requiring US$225 million in investment capital.

One large rubber concession in Laos was a reward for HAGL to build infrastructure for the 2009 SEA games in Vientiane.[8] HAGL also built a 200-bed hospital worth $6 million and presented it as a gift to the people of Attapeu. In return, HAGL was granted permission for a $100 million sugar and rubber processing factory. HAGL also built a new $300 million shopping mall in Yangon that opened in 2015. On the surface, while much of HAGL's access is likely a result of direct bribes to local officials, the company is also playing the role of patron, and even the state, in the provision of governance in the local area, mirroring classic Southeast Asian patronage politics (Scott 1972). Other regional land investments, such as within Cambodia, also have been linked to money laundering and elite corruption (Baird 2014).

3.3 Current Approaches to Meeting SDG 15

The primary actions that have been planned or taken to meet SDG 15 in Southeast Asia include establishment of PAs, restoration and rehabilitation of forest land, and certification schemes for sustainable commodities. Many of these conventional actions follow paths laid down over the past several decades to encourage Southeast Asian countries to sign multilateral agreements on the environment and establish national laws, but these legal approaches have often found minimal funding and weak enforcement. Designation of conservation zones has been uneven; marine areas remain underrepresented (see Section 4), as do wetlands, and recognizing local rights and equity has encountered difficulties. Reforestation and afforestation are priorities in places like Thailand, the Philippines, and Vietnam, but this has often depended on plantations of exotic acacia (a cheap, fast-growing species) at the expense of natural forests (McElwee and Nghi 2021).

---

[7] www.bloomberg.com/news/2011-03-23/hoang-anh-gia-lai-raises-56-5-million-with-london-gdr-listing.html.
[8] Financial Times. 2010. Hoang Anh Gia Lai builds its brand outside Vietnam, September 9.

Other actions aimed at the underpinning drivers of forest loss, such as shifting to more sustainable commodity production, have remained inadequate, dwarfed by the scale of the problems.

3.3.1 Protected Areas

Protected areas are a widely used approach to conserving ecosystems, and not a new phenomenon. Colonial powers created PAs when concerned about declining resource availability or to preserve resources for exclusive use (McElwee 2002). Every country in Southeast Asia has a system of legally designated PAs, although only Brunei and Cambodia have met a goal for 30 percent land coverage as prioritized in the recent GBF adopted in 2022 (Table 1). Across the region, an average of 14 percent of total lands are covered by nearly 1,400 PAs, including for terrestrial, freshwater, and marine systems.

PAs can slow biodiversity loss and contribute to conservation when they are well-managed and provide benefits to nearby communities (Brodie et al. 2023; Graham et al. 2021b). However, many PAs in Southeast Asia are "paper parks" only, with minimal management and serious problems with resource degradation.

Table 1 Protected areas coverage in Southeast Asia

Country	Total number of PAs (marine and terrestrial)	Terrestrial PAs as % of total land area	% of the terrestrial land area under PAs rated as having effective management[9]
Brunei Darussalam	56	46%	0%
Cambodia	69	39%	16%
Indonesia	733	12%	7%
Laos	35	19%	0%
Malaysia	528	13%	2%
Myanmar	53	6.5%	0.5%
Philippines	273	16%	2%
Singapore	4	6%	50%
Thailand	249	18.5%	7.5%
Timor-Leste	46	16%	0%
Vietnam	209	7.6%	7%

Source: www.protectedplanet.net/.

---

[9] In other words, protected areas that are not considered "paper parks" but that have financing and governance that is considered as least minimally effective.

Use of and residence within PAs is widespread, although considered illegal in many cases, which can lead to local conflicts, including poaching or arson. Reports on PAs often stress the need for more financial resources and capacity building (Graham et al. 2021a). Yet PAs cannot necessarily solve complex problems involving competing economic demands. For example, in Vietnam's Tam Dao National Park, provincial authorities granted permission to develop businesses even in the core zone, including a zoo, a train line, and a casino, despite protests by environmental NGOs. As the retired head of Vietnam's Park Service (who was himself opposed to these actions) told me, "The conflict between development and conservation is not easy to solve. For example, we have this strong movement to have 'ecotourism', and instead the companies build hotels, tennis courts etc. The leaders just don't understand the term." Some countries have tried to resolve this tension by taking a "fortress" approach to their PAs, building fences and excluding local communities, even if it is unrealistic and ineffective (McElwee 2002; Roth 2004).

Faced with poor management and isolation of many of the smaller PAs throughout Southeast Asia, some countries have turned to the idea of connectivity, through biodiversity corridors or transboundary PAs, to improve outcomes by expanding the size of PAs and the ability for species to move among them. For example, the Heart of Borneo Initiative between Brunei Darussalam, Indonesia, and Malaysia covers 30 percent of Borneo's land area and is supposed to be managed with joint decision-making (although evaluations suggest weak cooperation has happened to date), while the Greater Mekong Subregion countries have created biodiversity corridors since 2005 with support of the Asian Development Bank (ADB). However, the proposed corridors were drawn to exclude development interventions also being funded by the ADB, raising the question of how sustainable such plans really are (Box 4).

> **BOX 4 BIODIVERSITY CORRIDORS AS CAUTIONARY TALE**
>
> The countries of the Greater Mekong Subregion (GMS) meet regularly to propose ideas for collaborative and integrated development strategies, with projects coming out of these cooperative efforts often subsequently funded by the ADB. A key focus has been on economic corridors across countries, with major road networks linking Bangkok, Phnom Penh, and Ho Chi Minh City, and Yangon to Danang from east to west. Concurrent with interest in these economic corridors, the idea of biological corridors among the GMS countries was formally adopted in a 2005 resolution, supported by ADB development and funding of a Biodiversity Conservation Corridor Initiative (BCI). The project defined biodiversity conservation corridors (BCC) as

Box 4 (cont.)

"analogous to the economic corridors in their functionality and objectives, i.e., both attempt to increase the system connectivity, economies of scale, integration, and efficiency .... BCC allow the unhindered movement of species, and gains in scale efficiencies that are needed to sustain ecological processes that underpin sustainable development" (ADB 2004). Pilot projects were proposed in several GMS countries, including six such corridors with a total area of 130,000 hectares proposed across three provinces of Vietnam.

However, in order to proceed, there needed to be a legal basis for the concept of a BCC. An ongoing process from 2002 to 2008 to pass a Biodiversity Law in Vietnam provided the opportunity to introduce the concept to government officials and the public. Officials in the Ministry of Natural Resources and Environment (MONRE) were particularly targeted and they agreed to support both the ADB corridor project and the inclusion of the concept in the law. MONRE officials that I interviewed said that it sounded "useful for Vietnam," especially since the ADB was interested in funding a $30 million project for it. However, local areas where the corridors were to be located were less enthusiastic. One official involved with BCI noted,

> if there had been no money from the ADB, the provinces would not have gone to the trouble to do this . . . It's not coming from the province. The province says in meetings, we still don't have roads to go to work, why is there going to be a new corridor for animals? . . . We do it to make them [ADB] happy.

Why then did Vietnamese decision-makers become involved in a process in which many people confessed they did not understand? One stakeholder characterized it as an exchange, in which MONRE would include corridors in the national biodiversity law under development in return for money for implementation of the ADB project: "If the ADB had not given money to MONRE, they never would have thought about the biodiversity corridor." The fact that PAs themselves were not run by MONRE, but by another ministry, supported the idea that MONRE saw corridors as a chance to gain control over land management issues should the concept be introduced into law.

The planning process by the BCI to identify corridors was opaque: Mapping was done by technical consultants hired by the ADB and there were no public consultations or documents in Vietnamese available.

Box 4 (cont.)

Furthermore, the corridors proposed for Vietnam were drawn to exclude development interventions also being funded by the ADB. For example, the corridor connecting the Saola Nature Reserve and Song Thanh Nature Reserve in Central Vietnam went around a large hydropower dam, the Song Bung 4 dam, which at the time was under construction with ADB funding of $200 million. Even though there was forest in the area that was similar to the type proposed for the nearby corridor, it was not included because it was going to be flooded by reservoir construction. It was suggested by several interviewees that the ADB's interest in biodiversity corridors may have been driven not by objectives of conservation in the forefront, but as a public relations shield to deflect criticism of their extensive funding of road corridors and hydropower development.

3.3.2 Reforestation

Many country SDG plans include ambitious forest restoration projects, often aimed at the expansion of national forest cover or showcasing local tree planting efforts. For example, the Philippines' 2023 VNR highlighted a "1 Million Trees for 1 Bataan" project to cultivate shared responsibility for forestry, while Thailand's report focused on using corporate social responsibility efforts to expand tree cover, including investments made by the Electricity Generating Authority of Thailand. Forest landscape restoration involving smallholders should combine attention to livelihoods with provisioning of ecosystem services, but major barriers to participation have included insecure land tenure, competition with agriculture, and poor governance and corruption (McElwee and Nghi 2021).

Vietnam is a particularly useful cautionary tale. Several sizable tree planting and restoration programs over the past thirty years expanded forest cover from a low point of 9.4 Mha in 1990 to an estimated 14.6 Mha in 2020, although tree planting has been offset by continued loss in natural forests due to encroachment, illegal exploitation, fire, or other reasons (Cochard et al. 2017). Recent policies have encouraged the expansion of market activities and infrastructure like roads, forest product processing, and factories, aiming to diversify forest actors beyond the traditional role of the state. Much of the planting work is carried out by smallholder households, who now control somewhere between 40 and 70 percent of the country's production forests and generate at least US$500 million a year (McElwee and Nghi 2021). However, these reforestation efforts resulted in a shift toward exotic tree species, and ecosystem benefits from this greening have been low, particularly when monocrop tree plantations are harvested on short-term cycles. Acacia plantations alone now comprise 15–20 percent of total land area in some provinces (Tran et al. 2020a). There are also indications of gender impacts, as women's interests in tree planting often focus on multifunctional agroforestry, food security, and fuelwood production, which have tended to be de-emphasized in reforestation projects, while men have sought out income increasing opportunities. Overall, these tree planting projects have offered low value, few social benefits, and little ecological restoration potential, with insufficient attention to long-term sustainability for both people and forests (McElwee and Nghi 2021).

3.3.3 Market-Based Management of Ecosystems

Other strategies to meet SDG 15 have included market-based economic incentives: Examples include payments for environmental services (PES), forest carbon markets, and certification and labeling, such as shade-grown coffee or deforestation-free palm oil. PES aims to use payments from users of ecosystem services (like downstream water) to those who protect the areas that supply these benefits (e.g., in upstream forests). Reduced Emissions from Deforestation and Degradation (REDD+) policies use payments for carbon stocks to conserve forests, with funds raised from climate-concerned donors as well as private companies in voluntary carbon markets. The Norwegian Development Agency pledged $1 billion to Indonesia, giving them regional leader status for REDD+ projects, with other funding going to Vietnam, Cambodia, and Laos, and only smaller amounts to other countries. In Indonesia, projects are concentrated on the islands of Borneo and Sumatra, where forest loss has been most rapid and extensive (Graham et al. 2016). However, most REDD+ projects have suffered from a lack of clear understanding of the key agents of deforestation are (whether cash crop expansion, logging, corruption, or lack of enforcement) (McElwee 2016a; Milne 2012).

Local experience of these forest carbon projects is mixed; very little money has flowed for conservation on the ground, as the amount of preparatory work and technical requirements are very high. In one commune in Vietnam that has seen numerous consultants going in and out for meetings, carbon assessments and other readiness activities, a local leader coopted the REDD+ acronym, stating that in Vietnamese it actually stood for *"Roi Em Den va Di,"* which translates to "Here you come and go again" (McElwee 2016a). In other cases, rights to forests and responsibilities of forest-using peoples and their participation have not been well-addressed (Milne 2012). As a result, many REDD+ projects have primarily proceeded in a top-down fashion, paying little attention to structural changes that may be needed across economic sectors, and with limited participation of civil society or Indigenous Peoples that might be affected or serve to benefit (Maraseni et al. 2020).

Other market-based approaches have included certification and labeling and zero deforestation pledges. Forest certification is increasingly widespread, including an "ASEAN Timber Certification Scheme" to promote the acceptability of timber from the region and to ensure continued access to European markets, leading to patchworks of policies and approaches, such as EU-certified forests next to lands logged by the military in Laos (Barney 2012). Coffee certification, including shade-grown and biodiversity friendly standards, is also in use, but the majority sold from Vietnam and Indonesia, the two major players in the region, remains conventionally produced. Sustainable palm oil has also been promoted, but only covers about 20 percent of the market, and the process of certification favors large plantations who can afford certification (Box 2). An EU Deforestation Regulation that passed in 2023 to prevent imports of commodities implicated in deforestation has caused great concern across the region, with unclear implications for both smallholders and larger exporters (Warren-Thomas et al. 2023).

3.4 Alternative Approaches to the SDGs

Given the challenges in achieving sustainable development for the land sector from current policies, what might be some alternative approaches to addressing SDG 15? In other regions, expanded Indigenous rights to land, decentralization of PA management, and other more justice-centered approaches have provided evidence that community-centered conservation can help ensure benefits for both local people and biodiversity (Bridgewater et al. 2015; Krauss 2021). Accordingly, increased local access and power over decision-making through rights-based approaches has gained some steam in Southeast Asia as well; these often center local and Indigenous peoples' formal ownership and management of territories, or provide mechanisms for comanagement with other actors, like state agencies. These are not new approaches: Community-based forest management was a particularly popular trend in the late 1990s. However, these earlier experiments often had mixed results, due in part to incomplete decentralization, lack of understanding of local livelihoods, failures to address trends in commodity expansion that often competed for lands, and few explicit goals for equity and justice (Li 2002; Royer et al. 2018).

Recent support for designation of ICCAs provides a more durable way to recognize traditional land rights and achieve conservation successes with lower costs, as ICCAs often have better track records than state-managed PAs (Tran et al. 2020b). Ranging from small sacred forests to large-scale landscapes, ICCAs reflect values of nature held by different communities and often combine conservation with food provisioning, water supply protection, and other benefits. Because they are grounded in local beliefs, values, and histories, these zones, when self-generated, tend to be more successful at resisting pressures for land conversion. An ICCA Consortium for Southeast Asia was recently founded in 2018, although Indigenous communities have been advocating for territorial recognition for far longer (Conlu et al. 2022). Only two countries officially recognize ICCAs – Indonesia and the Philippines – although communities elsewhere have set them up anyway (see Figure 4). One example is the Salween Peace Park in Myanmar, with more than 500,000 hectares area of forest managed by the Karen Indigenous community; establishment has been a form of resistance to Burmese military control and a political statement that calls on other countries to recognize the Karen's rights (Paul et al. 2023).

Other forms of conservation rooted in Indigenous and local knowledge systems are found across the region. For example, the Karen community of Hid Lan Nai in northern Thailand has been recognized for restoring forest lands that had been previously logged as well as conserving species and genetic crop diversity (Figure 5), while elsewhere in Thailand, Buddhist monks have combined ritual activities with fire watches in community forests (Thammanu et al. 2021). Agricultural landscapes that combine food production and conservation are also important examples of community-based integrated management; for example, in Bali, the *subak* system combines rice terraces and canals with water temples that have been managed cooperatively for centuries under the concept of *Tri Hiti Karana*, a Balinese belief system regarding the interconnectedness of people, nature, and the spirit world (Risna et al. 2022). However, only around 9 percent of lands traditionally managed by Indigenous peoples in Asia are legally recognized, and some countries such as Laos and Vietnam do not recognize Indigenous claims to land at all (AIPP et al. 2022). Formalizing access to environmental justice to ensure rights-based approaches requires both access to information and strong rule of law. However, courts in Southeast Asia have not been key players in requiring distributive justice for environmental harms, as they have been in other regions, like Latin America.

Worryingly, recent deaths of environmental defenders in Laos, Cambodia, and Philippines, many of whom have been Indigenous, confirm the hostility of some states (Dressler and Smith 2023; Tran 2024); for example, in Thailand, a recently appointed chief of the National Parks service was suspected in the murder of an Indigenous Karen activist.[10] Women in particular have been targeted in some instances, creating a chilling effect for activists (Tran 2024).

---

[10] Bangkok Post. 2023. Former national park chief cleared of murder. September 28.

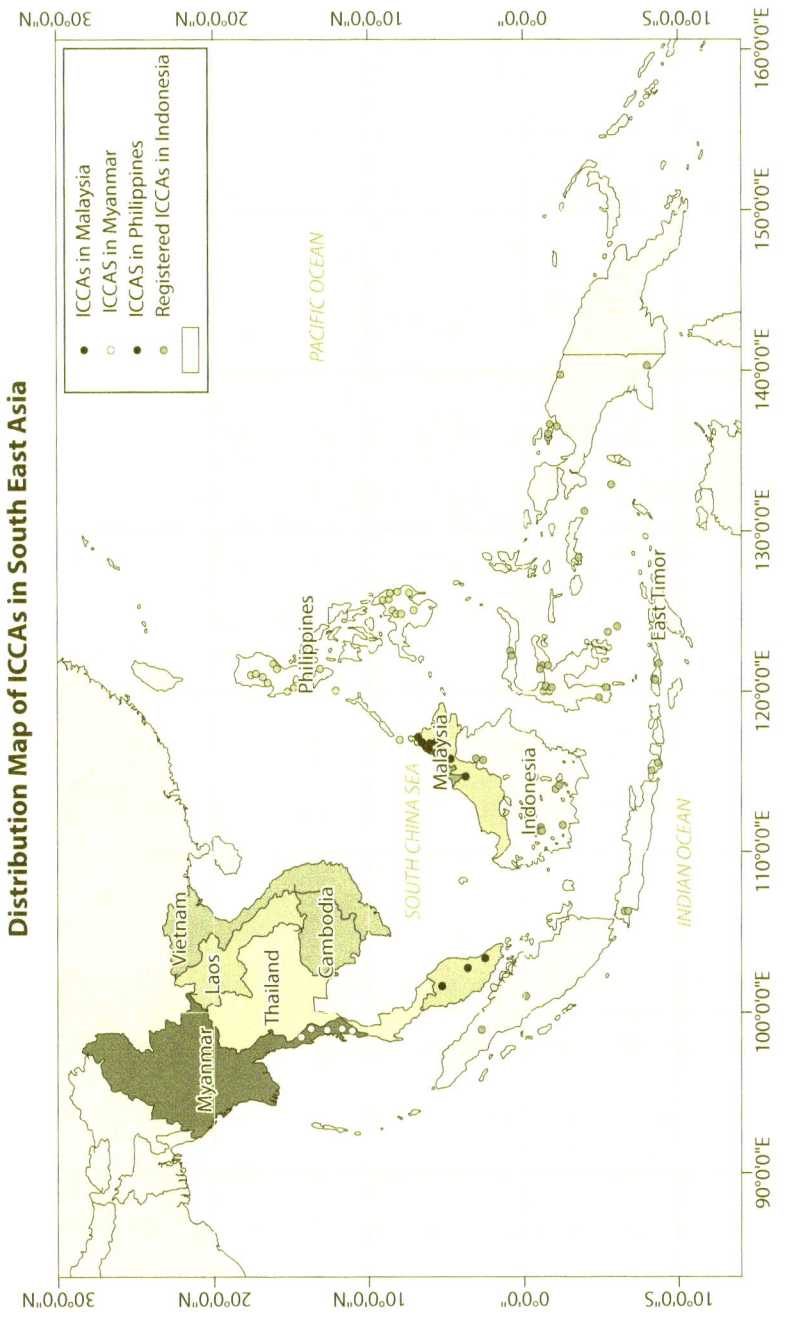

Figure 4 ICCAs in Southeast Asia. Additional ICCAs in Indonesia not yet recognized can be found in Sumatra and Borneo in particular and are indicated by boundary lines.

Source: Conlu et al. (2022).

Figure 5 Community-based biodiversity conservation in Hid Lan Nai, Thailand
Source: Photo by author, 2023.

It is also useful to examine what alternative solutions have not been proposed to meet SDG 15; for example, banning land conversion or speculation in land investments has not yet been suggested. Instead, some limited attention to improved land titling has occurred in response to land grabbing. For example, in Myanmar, the short-lived democratic regime in the late 2010s allowed space for civil society organizations to successfully organize against an overly general land law that would not have accounted for local conceptions of land in ethnic minority areas, while participatory inputs in Laos to land laws were also pursued by local communities, before eventually being bypassed by state actors seeking more investment-friendly land requirements (Kenney-Lazar et al. 2023).

There are also missed opportunities to link land use management more explicitly to health outcomes as part of improving the integration of policies across sectors. This includes increasing awareness of health risks from infectious diseases after COVID-19, as well as the hazards facing rubber and oil palm workers who have seen declines in productivity from diseases caused by land clearance (Morand and Lajaunie 2021; Shah et al. 2019), and heat exposure and stress (Wolff et al. 2021). Experimental projects to provide improved health care to communities near the Gunung Palung National Park in Indonesia in return for reduced logging pressures have shown promise (Webb et al. 2018). The growing concern by middle classes regarding air pollution, often caused by transboundary haze as a result of land burning, also presents an opportunity. In northern Thailand, as haze from burning agricultural residues in the spring has impacted air travel and lead to spikes in respiratory illnesses, Thai citizens have protested and filed lawsuits with the Prime Minister's office for failing to take the problem seriously.[11] Their claims of a right to clean air may serve to spur more rights-based approaches elsewhere.

3.5 Conclusions

Numerous attempts over the past several decades to increase sustainable use of lands and waters have not stopped degradation trends in Southeast Asia. All too often, singular objectives for provisioning of export goods (timber, oil palm, rubber, or food) have dominated over alternative pathways. There has been a lack of attention to integration across ecosystems in multifunctional interventions, such as reforestation that also supplies food and water, or PAs that have both conservation and social justice aims. While PAs have slowed some degradation, when they have not been aligned with local support or have been driven by outside actors, as was the case with conservation corridors in the Mekong, these have been less effective and often come at the expense of local livelihoods. Thus, more widespread benefits might be possible with locally directed and supported efforts centered in rights-based approaches, such as in ICCAs. Some market-based schemes like REDD+ or PES have tried to establish financial parity with global commodity pressures, but these approaches have not been able to balance equitable benefit sharing with inclusive development processes. Other market-based approaches like certification remain limited to small percentages of marketed goods, and often favoring large-scale producers who can manage checklists of formal requirements, while smallholders who would most benefit most remain excluded.

The closed political systems within some countries also limit the amount of space and agency for civil society to advocate for more equitable and integrated solutions to improve the situation (Gritten et al. 2019). Given limited engagement of different knowledge systems, including those of Indigenous communities, it is not a surprise that most countries have focused on technocratic policies, instead of more multifunctional, co-beneficial, and inclusive approaches. Overall, SDG 15 fails to provide an overarching theory of change

---

[11] Wanli, Y. 2024. Thailand ponders measures against burgeoning haze crisis. *China Daily*, January 18.

as to how Southeast Asia might balance competing demands for resources, and governance challenges related to integration, equity, and accountability have stymied more progressive solutions to date.

4 Life Below Water: Marine and Coastal Ecosystems

4.1 Introduction

As one of the great maritime regions of the world, Southeast Asia faces pressing problems in balancing protection of key ecosystems like coral reefs, coastal mangroves, and the open sea with pressures from commercial aquaculture and fisheries (ASEAN 2017). Nearly 40 percent of the world's mangroves are located here, and a third of total coral reefs, including the Coral Triangle, considered the world hot spot of marine biodiversity. These rich ecosystems supply livelihoods, food, and water to hundreds of millions, as well as protection from storms and floods, sequestration of carbon, and recreational opportunities (Figure 6). Nearly 80 percent of the region's population lives near these coastal zones, requiring that marine ecosystems be managed for multifunctional benefits, from traditional small-scale fisher livelihoods to large-scale ocean energy exploitation (ASEAN 2021).

Figure 6 Coastal Lombok and Mount Agung, Bali, Indonesia
Source: Photo by author.

Once seen as a limitless frontier, there is increasingly visible evidence of harm, including rising temperatures and sea levels caused by climate change, hypoxia (deoxygenation) from nutrient pollution, plastic debris from poor waste management, and overfishing that is decreasing fish size, type, and availability (Ferrol-Schulte et al. 2015; Omeyer et al. 2022; Todd et al. 2010). SDG 14 targets for "life under water" focus on the need to manage and restore marine ecosystems and increase conservation areas; to manage fisheries sustainably, including the elimination of subsidies that contribute to overfishing; to reduce marine pollution; and to address consequences of climate change. Yet currently all countries of Southeast Asia that have access to coasts (i.e., excluding Laos) are failing on the most basic indicators of ocean health, let alone implementing more complex policies to sustainably manage and protect marine and coastal ecosystems. This section focuses on three primary areas of needed action: mangrove and coral reef ecosystems and drivers of degradation related to aquaculture expansion, particularly export-shrimp booms; management of capture fisheries in marine and freshwater bodies, which are currently overexploited and associated with social conflicts and poverty; and ocean and marine pollution, for which Southeast Asia is a global hot spot.

4.2 Drivers of Change

Mangroves and coral reefs are both crucial economic and ecological systems within Southeast Asia. Mangroves provide timber, firewood, charcoal, tannin, food, and medicines, and serve as reservoirs of biodiversity and carbon. Both mangroves and reefs play a hugely important role in protecting coastlines and riverbanks from coastal erosion and storm damage; the value of this protection for the Philippines alone is estimated at more than US$1 billion per year (Menéndez et al. 2018). Despite their economic contributions, more than 80 percent of Southeast Asia reefs are degraded or at risk, including more than 90 percent of Indonesia's coral reefs, while in Vietnam, only 1 percent of coral reefs are in good condition (Ferrol-Schulte et al. 2015; Todd et al. 2010). The loss or degradation of coastal ecosystems over the past half century has been driven primarily by economic development: For mangroves, land use change has converted these rich ecosystems into intensive aquacultural or agricultural fields (Friess et al. 2019; Richards and Friess 2016), while for coral reefs, urban expansion, pollution and runoff from coasts, overfishing, and excess tourism have all affected their health (Heery et al. 2018).

The primary driver of mangrove loss has been aquaculture expansion, setting up a clash between national economic development plans and the benefits of maintaining natural ecosystems along coasts (Figure 7). Mangrove conversion

(a)

(b)

Figure 7 Risks to Mangroves
(a) Restored mangrove area in Can Gio, Vietnam at risk of development;
(b) Shrimp pond in converted mangroves near Xuan Thuy National Park, Vietnam.

Source: Photos by author 2009, 2019.

accelerated from the late 1970s through the 2000s due to booming global demand for shrimp (Hall 2003; Vandergeest et al. 1999). Between 1980 and 2005, the global extent of mangrove forests declined by 20 percent, with just six Southeast Asian countries (Indonesia, Myanmar, Malaysia, the Philippines, Thailand, and Vietnam) accounting for 80 percent of all human-driven losses (Goldberg et al. 2020). Southeast Asia accounts for almost 89 percent of global aquaculture production, generating an estimated $10 billion per year (FAO 2018). Vietnam is now the world's number two exporter of shrimp, and Thailand number three.

Aquaculture development has benefited from both government promotion and private incentives (Akber et al. 2020). For example, in Vietnam, state policies encouraged household ownership of coastal lands as the country decollectivized in the late 1980s, with the area for shrimp farming rapidly expanding from 250,000 hectares in 2000 to more than 600,000 hectares by 2005 (Cao 2007). In Thailand, a Thai multinational conglomerate, CP Group, has played an important role to encourage smallholders to intensify productivity of shrimp through verticalization (e.g., supplying inputs to producers and expecting in turn for shrimp to be sold back up the supply chain) (Goss et al. 2000). Boom and bust cycles for shrimp – with some producers making a killing while others are left impoverished and indebted – has contributed to rising inequality, including between men and women, as the latter lost harvesting rights as formerly commonly managed mangroves and mudflats were converted in Vietnam (Le 2021).

Fisheries, like mangroves, are also in various states of degradation, with poor management of fishing stocks and overfishing (Teh and Pauly 2018). Southeast Asia generates around 25 percent of the world's total fish production, and 30 million people work directly in the fishing sector, with a wider population of 150 million in associated businesses like processing or boat construction, making this the most fishing-dependent region of the globe (Pomeroy et al. 2016). Subsistence, small-scale, and commercial fishing all compete and contribute to national incomes and household livelihoods, but most countries have overcapacity in terms of boats and gear, leading to conflicts and declining catch per unit effort (Suuronen et al. 2020). While some countries' overall catches have been rising, this is often due to increased effort and moving down the chain to smaller and less profitable species (Pomeroy et al. 2016). In the Philippines, fisheries have seen catches decrease, leading to a 250 percent increase in individual effort over the past fifty years (Selgrath et al. 2018). Limited alternative livelihoods and lack of enforcement of existing fishing regulations have often pushed fishers to catch more for fear that someone else will do so if they do not.

Illegal, unreported, and unregulated (IUU) fishing is also a major problem: Violations include fishing in PAs or other countries' territorial waters, deactivating ship monitoring systems, using false flags, or moving transshipments at sea rather than specified landing ports (Chapsos and Hamilton 2019). Between 3.5 and 8 million tons of fish are estimated to be caught as a result of IUU fishing each year in the broader Asia–Pacific region (APEC 2014), and are valued at $23 billion (Wilcox et al. 2021). Regional hot spots of IUU are found along Vietnam's coastal boundary and in the Celebes Sea between Philippines and Indonesia (Wilcox et al. 2021). The problem is complex, involving disputed waters and asymmetry between countries on enforcement, compounded by fish buyers as drivers and a lack of involvement of the private sector in solutions (Wilcox et al. 2021). Recent exposes of the fishing industry have also revealed problems of unsafe working conditions and even slavery (EJF 2019b; Marschke and Vandergeest 2016).

Much of the incentive to overfish or fish illegally comes from strong global demand in the EU, United States, Japan, China, and elsewhere; margins for fishers and processors are thin, and overfishing helps meet these demands. The seafood industry has also consolidated, with just thirteen corporations controlling up to 40 percent of the largest and most valuable fish stocks (Österblom et al. 2015), leading to widening inequality as small fishers are squeezed on prices paid. Asia also has the highest government subsidies for fisheries in the world (nearly half of all global subsidies), and this $15 billion per year is strongly implicated in overfishing (Sumaila et al. 2016). Subsidies have been used to build capacity or exploit new areas (such as moving from inshore to offshore) through subsidization of bigger boats or fuel. This has resulted in higher pressures on many stocks; in Vietnam, for example, nearly 50 percent of fish stocks are estimated to be fully exploited, overexploited, or near collapse, in part due to high subsidies and low enforcement of regulations (Harper and Sumaila 2019; Ho and Ngo 2023). Overall, evidence suggests that larger fishing boat owners, rather than small-scale fishers, have benefited from these subsidies (Pham et al. 2021). For small fishers, all too often fishing is not a pathway out of poverty but rather a difficult and low-status occupation, requiring long trips away from home on cramped vessels, or undertaken only as a supplement to more stable income sources (Stobutzki et al. 2006) (Figure 8).

Both coastal mangroves and marine fisheries are both affected by rising pollution as well, from plastic pollution, run-off of fertilizers and pesticides, dredging and mining (both on land and in the sea), rapid expansion of coastal cities and industrial development, and poor waste management (Heery et al. 2018; Lu et al. 2018; Tran and Nguyen 2019) (see Box 5). Many countries still allow untreated sewage to be dumped, such as Bangkok into the Gulf of Thailand and the city of Manila into Manila Bay (Sotto et al. 2015). In turn, these pollutants affect human health, particularly via toxic algal blooms or

Figure 8 Traditional small-scale fishing boats in Nha Trang harbor, Vietnam
Source: Photo by author, 2001.

BOX 5 FISH VERSUS STEEL IN VIETNAM

On April 6, 2016, hundreds of thousands of dead fish began to wash up on a 200-km stretch of coast in central Vietnam. Suspicion soon fell on the largest steel-making complex in Southeast Asia, a US$10 billion plant built by the Taiwanese firm Formosa Plastics Group. The government's initial response was bungled, with authorities from the Department of Fisheries, Ministry of Health, and Prime Minister's office giving out different possible explanations, eventually settling on the idea that the fish kill was the result of a toxic algal bloom and unrelated to Formosa. Yet on April 25, a statement from the director of the factory that Vietnam had to choose between catching fish and building a modern steel industry made it clear that something was indeed amiss. On April 27, the deputy minister of MONRE gave a statement that government tests had determined what the pollution was, but the information would not be shared with the public. (Only later was it revealed that untreated waste had been released from the plant, containing cyanide, phenol, and iron hydroxides.)

Starting April 28, residents in the four affected central provinces were banned from fishing and could not sell even those fish they had caught and frozen earlier in the season, leaving more than half a million people out of business (Truong et al. 2021). The bumbling and opaque response from authorities only served to fire up both online dissent and physical protests, which spontaneously began on May 1 and continued throughout the summer. Hundreds of families protested along roadways by throwing dead fish at passing cars. Organized protests also occurred in Hanoi and Ho Chi Minh City, as well as regional cities like Danang and Hue. Protestors held up signs stating "*Toi chon ca* [I choose fish]" or "*Ca can nuoc sach; dan can minh bach*

Box 5 (cont.)

[Fish need clean water; people need transparency]" (Figure 9). By the following weekend, at least 3,000 people turned out in both cities, and authorities responded with mass arrests of several hundred people. Facebook began to be blocked sporadically starting in May, leading many to speculate it was to prevent further organizing of protests. Avant-garde fish "die-ins" were staged by artists in Hue, while pop artists wrote songs talking about fish, and in this way, the protests became a broad based, multi-class social movement.

By June 2016, government authorities officially laid blame on Formosa in a letter requesting compensation, and by end of the month, they stated they had received a payment of US$500 million that would be used to quickly compensate affected people. In reality, the money went to households one to two years later, around US$4,000 each in total, although it was too late and too little for most (Truong et al. 2021). An official at the Fisheries Department confirmed to me that it was Formosa who suggested $500 million in payment, and that the government had done no assessment to determine actual damages. Even close to a decade later, no studies have been published examining the effects of the spill on coastal ecosystems due to restrictions on access by the government (Dinh 2019).

Figure 9 Hanoi protest against the Formosa pollution on May 1, 2016
Source: Facebook.

Box 5 (cont.)

During the summer of 2016, very few formal environmental NGOs took positions on either the pollution or the compensation proposed by the government, fearing government reprisals. It was other civic associations, such as the Catholic Church, LGBT groups, and local age and school cohort associations that came together to protest the way families were treated. Catholic priests helped families file lawsuits against Formosa in local courts, with more than 500 filed by September, but these were summarily rejected on the grounds that the government was already providing compensation. One local district rejected the government settlement offer and stated they should enter into direct negotiations with Formosa, since they were the most affected and should present claims for damages directly. In October 2016, an estimated 20,000 residents gathered outside the Formosa factory to continue their protests, while more protests in February 2017 were met with a heavy police presence and reports of beatings and arrests. After failing to pursue the case in Vietnamese courts, 8,000 citizens filed suit in Taiwan in 2019 claiming additional damages, but the case is still tied up in technicalities. Recent surveys of Vietnamese citizens indicate that most reject the framing of fish versus steel and do not want to sacrifice the environment for development, expressing willingness to accept lower levels of economic growth in exchange for higher environmental protection (Nguyen and Malesky 2021).

contaminated marine products, harm biodiversity, and create trade-offs with other economic sectors, like tourism (Todd et al. 2010). Harmful algal blooms (HABs, also sometimes known as red tides) are the result of nutrient pollution creating excess phytoplankton which decomposes, and have occurred regularly in Southeast Asia since the 1970s, with the Philippines and Malaysia the two primary hot spots. Toxins produced by HABs can contaminate shellfish and lead to both fish kills and to human death if consumed, requiring shellfish advisories and close monitoring (Yñiguez et al. 2021). The problem of plastic waste is also a key sustainability issue: Much of the waste is carried from inland rivers to oceans, and Southeast Asia contributes around 30 percent of the global ocean plastics problem, with Indonesia, Philippines, Vietnam, Thailand, and Malaysia being the main culprits (Jambeck et al. 2015). The Brantas, Solo, Serayu, and Progo rivers in Indonesia; the Irrawaddy in Myanmar; the Pasig in the Philippines; and the transboundary Mekong are among the top twenty global sources of plastic pollution (Lebreton et al. 2017).

4.3 Current Approaches to Meeting SDG 14

All these pressures on coastal and marine ecosystems underscore the urgency of sustainable development. However, attempts to address coastal land conversion, overfishing, and excess pollution have been mostly piecemeal to date, with insufficient funding and support, and rarely addressing the deeper drivers and causes of the problem. Trade-offs between the achievement of SDG 14 and SDG 2, on food security, or SDG 8, on economic growth, are very real. For the recovery of coral reefs and overfished marine populations, MPAs are a predominant strategy, while for coastal systems, mangrove protection and restoration programs have been pursued. Policy solutions proposed have tended to be a mix of state-dominated regulatory efforts, although often insufficiently small, with some use of market-based incentives like seafood certification. Other promising options, like community management of MPAs, have remained mostly localized and small-scale.

4.3.1 Protected Areas and Marine and Coastal Conservation

SDG Target 14.5 calls for the conservation at least 10 percent of coastal and marine areas, but every Southeast Asian nation is falling far short of this. Approximately 600 MPAs have been gazetted across Southeast Asia, but they are relatively small (Cros et al. 2014), and like terrestrial PAs, many exist on paper only, with few having concrete management plans or sufficient funding (Kamil et al. 2017; White et al. 2014). MPAs have been more effective in countries with low capacity, primarily because they are easier to put in place than other types of regulations that require more complex enforcement (e.g., for IUU) (Turschwell et al. 2020). In general, where local communities have been involved in negotiations over boundaries and in benefit-sharing, there is more acceptance of MPAs and increased benefits (Savage et al. 2020; Teh et al. 2013).

Globally, most high-priority mangroves areas that need protection are in Asia (75 percent of needs) (Dabalà et al. 2023). However, only around 7 percent of Southeast Asia's mangroves are currently protected, and that number is skewed by higher protection in Philippines and Indonesia, while other countries have virtually no protective status whatsoever (Friess et al. 2016). While Indonesia and the Philippines have benefited from high-level attention and longer histories of recognition of the benefits of mangroves, there still remain challenges. For example, in Indonesia, mangroves are addressed by twenty-two different laws and eighteen competing agencies, with similar examples in Thailand and the Philippines, leading to policy overlap and incoherence (Friess et al. 2016). Even formal protection does not prevent land conversion: For example, the Red River Delta Biosphere Reserve in Vietnam is experiencing major encroachment for aquaculture (Figure 7b), and local provincial authorities have been hoping to degazette mangroves to enable them to be converted to a golf course and economic development zone (Tatarski 2023).

Actions to regulate overfishing and end illegal fishing (Target 14.4) and to reduce fisheries subsides (Target 14.6) have had little success (Ferrol-Schulte et al. 2015). Although nearly all Southeast Asian countries have regulatory measures, including banning destructive practices like explosives or cyanide fishing, as well as closed seasons and areas and allowable catch limits (Kotowicz et al. 2022), enforcement and compliance remain poor. Most of the coastal Southeast Asian countries have signed various agreements on IUU, and pressure from outside the region is important in governance efforts as well. The EU has threatened to ban Thai fish from being imported unless Thailand deals with overfishing and slavery issues (Derrick et al. 2017), while Vietnam was issued a yellow card by the European Commission against wild-caught seafood exports (EJF 2019a). Reducing overcapacity ("too many fishers chasing too few fish") requires difficult political choices, through catch reduction by having fewer fishers (e.g., buying back boats or gear to reduce their use) or limits to amount caught (Pomeroy 2012; Salayo et al. 2008). Effort reduction policies (e.g., closed seasons or gear restrictions) can be more acceptable, depending on implementation, but overall, there are no magic bullets to resolve the overcapacity problems (Bush and Marschke 2016).

4.3.2 Market-Based Policies for Ecosystems and Fisheries

Recent years have brought increased funding and interest to large-scale mangrove restoration as a "nature-based solution" for climate mitigation and adaptation (Saunders et al. 2020). In 2020, Indonesian President Joko Widodo announced ambitions to plant 600,000 hectares of mangroves within five years. Organizations like Mangroves for the Future and the Global Mangrove Alliance have promoted restoration projects, often touting the economic benefits; for example, every $1 million invested in mangrove rehabilitation in northern Vietnam is estimated to save over $7 million annually in dyke maintenance costs (Brown et al. 2006), while the value of rehabilitated mangroves to villages in coastal Java is estimated at over US$2000 per household per year (Damastuti and Groot 2017).

However, if the drivers of mangrove decline are not tackled, restoration projects face the same pressures for conversion (Gerona-Daga and Salmo 2022) (Box 6).

Box 6 Lessons Learned from Mangrove Restoration in Vietnam

In 1943 there were an estimated 430,000 hectares of mangroves in Vietnam, but nearly 40 percent of were destroyed by US herbicides during the Vietnam War (Van et al. 2015). After the war's close, the shrimp boom hit Vietnam, reducing mangrove area even further to less than 150,000 hectares in the early 2000s (Veettil et al. 2019). Mangrove restoration has been encouraged and funded through multiple sources in recent years, including donors and the Vietnam Red Cross, often driven by interest in disaster risk reduction (Kumar et al. 2015). Vietnam's Nationally Determined Contribution (NDC) to the Paris Agreement in 2016 made a pledge to add 20,000–50,000 hectares of restored and afforested mangroves in recognition of their high carbon benefits.

Both manually planted and naturally regenerated mangroves have shown the possibilities, yet also the limits, of restoration success (Nam et al. 2016). A common model has been to encourage mangrove restoration within mixed shrimp production ponds by smallholders with per hectare forest planting incentives plus longer-term payments for protection, as well as allocating protection forest (on which 70 percent forest cover must be retained) for management by households. However, these models have been complicated by land tenure issues, because many households taking part hold yearly contracts with a State Forest Company (which officially owns the land), limiting households' decision-making power. Consequently, some households have even wanted to return allocated lands back to the government. In another complication, the subsidies for restoration provided incentives for destruction due to poor monitoring; in Kien Giang province, participants actually cut existing mangroves down to replace them with seedlings in order to receive the subsidy, thereby leading to loss of mature diverse forests (Phong et al. 2017).

Restoration success has also been dependent on what was planted and where. In Kien Giang, use of *Rhizophora apiculata* by reforestation projects replaced a more diverse mangrove ecology, leading to less resilience and increased coastal erosion as *Rhizophora* roots were less deep-rooted and could not withstand strong wave action (Phong et al. 2017). A different donor-funded afforestation project in the same province was more successful by using local ideas of low-cost fencing to ensure mangrove survival (Nguyen et al. 2016). However, pressures on mangroves have not abated given the opportunity cost of reforestation versus continued shrimp production. This has led some donors to advocate for "blue carbon" financing from

> Box 6 (cont.)
>
> international carbon markets, and some willingness-to-pay studies have shown that smallholders appreciate the storm reduction benefits provided by mangroves if they are compensated to retain these (Pham et al. 2018). However, such approaches have been in theory only; the Ministry of Agriculture and Rural Development was charged with defining and valuing mangrove ecosystem services way back in 2010, but a lack of clarity on who would be the buyers and sellers have prevented inclusion of either mangroves or carbon stocks in existing payments from ecosystem services policy (McElwee et al. 2019). Further, even successful restoration projects can remain threatened; the Can Gio mangrove biosphere reserve at the mouth of the Saigon River, reforested in the 1970s at the end of the Vietnam War, is currently being targeted for urban development as a residential suburb (Nguyen and Keeton-Olsen 2023).

Some restoration projects focused on single species have not succeeded in emulating the rich biodiversity of natural mangrove forests, nor involved local stakeholders (Camacho et al. 2020); accordingly low survival rates of less than 10 percent have occurred in some places. Restoration is also expensive: Replanting just one-third of Indonesia's target of 600,000 hectares will likely cost up to $2 billion US$ (Sasmito et al. 2023). Because restored mangroves have high carbon benefits, this has led to interest in using market incentives to provide funding. Voluntary carbon markets that allow companies to buy "offsets" to make up for their carbon emissions have attracted support, with Southeast Asia seen as an ideal place to incentivize this "blue carbon." Yet in reality, most countries have failed to create markets to pay for mangrove restoration or protection because they lack the necessary governance and enforcement mechanisms (Friess et al. 2016).

The most important market-based approach to address coastal and marine systems has been seafood certification, requiring producers to meet voluntary guidelines for sustainable production in return for a higher price premium. Thailand first experimented with shrimp certification in the 1990s, primarily driven by demands for traceability and quality assurance from importing countries like the EU, United States, and Japan. Private certification standards require different measures of environmental compliance, such as insuring no loss of mangroves or prohibiting use of antibiotics. Vietnam, with the largest area of shrimp ponds in the world, has been a prime testing ground. Ca Mau province in the Mekong Delta produces 25 percent of Vietnam's export shrimp and uses six different certification schemes depending on the destination (Ha et al. 2012a; Watanabe and Ubukata 2023). However, certification is limited to small areas and comprises less than 4 percent of the total global market, with 3 percent of shrimp in Vietnam and less than 1 percent in Indonesia and Thailand certified as sustainable (Davis and Boyd 2021). There is also high variability between standards on environmental or social requirements (Tran et al. 2013). Certification also usually favors larger producers, who can complete the burdensome compliance requirements, and which can serve to increase the power of larger industrial producers. For smallholders, more partnership between farmers, intermediaries like NGOs, and other actors working together (e.g., in clusters of farms or cooperatives) can improve success (Ha et al. 2013; Hatanaka 2010).

As with shrimp aquaculture, there has been interest in using certification and labeling to verify sustainable fisheries, with the Marine Stewardship Council (MSC) one of several standards. However, MSC has only certified a small number of sustainable fisheries in the developing world, and IUU practices in Southeast Asia have been a major barrier. The only currently certified fishery is found in Vietnam, where a clam cooperative that prohibits mechanization and restricts rake and net size has led to a 400 percent increase in prices paid for the 13,000 people involved (Blackmore et al. 2015). These and other measures have been labeled a "blue economy" approach, which treats oceans as a form of natural capital to draw businesses to marine zones and support market and technological development (Satizábal et al. 2020). However, these market-driven approaches have not been balanced with supply-side measures that tackle overfishing incentives and other key drivers (Pomeroy et al. 2016). Fisheries subsidies reform, for example, has not been addressed, and pressures during the COVID-19 pandemic increased government support to combat disruptions in supply chains, closures of markets, and decreases in income and tax revenue (FAO 2022). While short-term measures can help fishers' livelihoods, long-term subsidies are implicated in overfishing and often favor larger companies.

In other regions of the world, other market-based measures for fishing like tradable quotas have been more widely used, but they require strong enforcement mechanisms that are lacking in Southeast Asia, and there has been opposition and protest against full privatization of marine resources that change long-standing fishing traditions (Pomeroy 2012). Instead, some Southeast Asian countries have experimented with area-based "territorial use rights" (TURFs) which "partially or totally privatize fishing areas for groups of users" (Quynh et al. 2017) in the hopes of incentivizing better management of fish stocks and eliminating the common pool resource problem in fisheries. Vietnam has introduced TURFs, which have stabilized some conflicts but not yet led to reduced fishing pressures (Armitage et al. 2011; Ho et al. 2015). Factors leading to success include cross-TURF coordination groups, low pressure from illegal fishing by non-TURF members, and a well-defined ecological boundary, with low mobility of species (Quynh et al. 2017).

4.3.3 Pollution Policies

Mismanagement of solid waste, high population densities, and extensive rains and flooding all conspire to make the plastics problem in Southeast Asia difficult to address. Single use plastics are widespread, with low recycling rates regionally, although some bag bans are being adopted (Marks et al. 2020; Mathis et al. 2022). Singapore, a country with limited space and higher wealth, has improved to 60 percent of waste recycled and 38 percent incinerated; in contrast, Indonesia still landfills 70 percent, some of which ends up in waterways (Visvanathan and Anbumozhi 2018). The import of waste from Europe and the United States is also a major culprit, particularly after China banned plastic waste imports in 2017, leading the trade to move to other Asian countries. Blaming Southeast Asia for being the epicenter of marine plastics, yet not holding plastic manufacturers in the global North accountable for their production, highlights the unevenness of responsibility (Owens and Conlon 2021).

Southeast Asian countries have adopted a mix of regulatory and market-based approaches to combat marine pollution, mostly focused on general frameworks for action. For example, in Vietnam, recent laws provide targets for reduction of marine pollution and dumping at sea and a ban on disposable plastics by 2025 (Truong and Chu 2020), while Thailand's recent "Roadmap on Plastic Waste Management" has banned several types of plastic, and some Indonesian cities have instituted bag taxes. Basic approaches like raising awareness and requiring waste separation are important first steps (Mathis et al. 2022), but concerns have been raised that industrial actors from the petrochemical sector who want to continue to produce plastics often influence government decisions, such as in Thailand, where the sector contributes 7 percent of GDP (Marks et al. 2023).

Circular economy approaches have been proposed to reduce waste, keep materials in use, and reduce the need for new inputs. Singapore has a goal of net plastic circularity by 2030, alongside more tech-focused solutions, like installing booms on rivers to collect waste (Omeyer et al. 2022). However, most circular economy approaches in Southeast Asia are in name only and suffer from being based on Western models that ignore local solutions; for example, the important role of informal sector waste pickers and their perspectives have been ignored (Marks et al. 2023). True extended producer responsibility that would require businesses to be responsible for the life cycle of their products is not embedded in any laws in Southeast Asia.

4.4 Alternatives to Meeting SDG 14

As is the case for terrestrial ecosystem management, alternatives to the marine environment often foreground community-based management. These initiatives have often provided stricter enforcement (such as no-take rules that restrict any fishing), enforced through local customary norms (Christie et al. 2002; Selgrath et al. 2018). For example, in Indonesian systems known as *sasi*, fishers are prohibited from using destructive fishing methods and seasonal rules of entry and harvest are enforced (Harkes and Novaczek 2002). Elsewhere in Indonesia, community values, such as the Balinese concept of *"sad kerti,"* have helped inform strategies to maintain the balance of nature across spirits, human, ecosystems, and the universe, and have been included in local MPAs (Berdej and Armitage 2016). Rights-based approaches to MPAs show that it is possible to have biological success as well as community participation and benefits (Fidler et al. 2022). Key indicators of success have included sustainable financing, clarity of rules and enforcement, trust among users, and multistakeholder planning processes (Chaigneau and Daw 2015; Green et al. 2011).

Community-based management and restoration for mangroves can also be successful if they avoid some of the negative drivers seen in Box 6. Several projects in Indonesia and Thailand have foregrounded livelihood dependence on benefits and services from mangroves, undergirded by community regulations and financial support from states and donors (Damastuti and Groot 2017; Sudtongkong and Webb 2008; Triyanti et al. 2017). Other factors of success have included high levels of public support, garnered through inclusion and trust, larger spatial scales and ambitions backed by longer-term funding, and supportive regulatory environments with accountability and enforcement (Damastuti et al. 2022). Non-market ecosystem and cultural benefits have tended to be undervalued in restoration programs and could provide a useful framing for future projects (Gerona-Daga and Salmo 2022); examples include heritage, identity, and sense of place; aesthetic, spiritual, and inspirational values; recreation and education; and other relational benefits which provide incentives for protection (Gajardo et al. 2023). More attention to incorporating Indigenous and local knowledge into species selection and planting protocols is likely to be beneficial as well (Loch and Riechers 2021).

Comanagement of fisheries through increased roles for local communities has also shown success (Kotowicz et al. 2022). For example, a 1998 law in the

Philippines gave more rights to local communities in nearshore fisheries, which many have parlayed into sustainable initiatives (Selgrath et al. 2018). Where fishers have been given more rights, fishing associations have been able to self-organize, even among the most marginalized (Andriesse et al. 2022). Successful comanagement of fisheries shows that establishing clear rules for exploitation is crucial, as well as locally appropriate norms for compliance, alongside providing communal income streams (Prescott and Steenbergen 2017). However, all too often, the power to make rules is not truly devolved to fishing communities and remains on paper only, leading to diminished outcomes (Ho et al. 2015).

Environmental justice claims for use of ocean and coastal zones are also rising in importance, including the use of transnational courts and public protests, as seen in the Vietnam Formosa case. These efforts have joined unfamiliar partners through heavy use of social media and physical presence on the streets, leading to the emergence of a broad-based coalition of citizens of many stripes. Questions have been posed about how representative protest movements and civil society organizations are (Forsyth 2007): Are they primarily for and by the middle class, or can they reach out to poorer people who are often the most seriously impacted by degradation and disasters? In the Formosa case, the steel plant pollution touched on both food consumption safety for the middle class, and the importance of livelihoods for lower-class fishers. However, the degree to which the outpouring of support for stronger enforcement of pollution measures and less deference to economic development at any cost will influence future policies in Vietnam and elsewhere remains to be seen.

4.5 Conclusions

Marine and coastal systems in Southeast Asia remain highly stressed, and sustainability initiatives small and scattered. Where community-based natural resources management has been pursued, from mangrove restoration to MPAs, better social and environmental outcomes have resulted (Ha et al. 2012b; Pomeroy 1995). Yet top-down state management continues to be the norm, risking corruption and continued patron–client relationships, and policies that favor large actors (trawling fleets, seafood conglomerates) over smallholders and small fishers remains a key failing (Orchard et al. 2015). Using market-based policies to value coastal and marine systems has also been challenging; while they have drawn attention to the myriad benefits obtained from coastal ecosystems, attempts to financialize carbon and other blue economy markets have met roadblocks. Certification schemes have provided some benefits to both people and nature, but remain limited to very small shares of the global market. Cases like the Formosa fish kill point out the need for regular environmental monitoring, stricter pollution regulations, and transparency: basic components of environmental protection in place in North America and Europe, but often missing in Southeast Asia.

As was the case for terrestrial policies examined in the previous section, there is a lack of integrated approaches across ecosystems, sectors, and countries for holistic marine policies and approaches. Yet these interconnections are inescapable; for example, IUU fishing can often produce low-quality trash fish, which are then used to generate fishmeal to feed shrimp in ponds in cleared mangroves, supplied in plastic bags that end up in the ocean and polluting fishing grounds. It is difficult to reduce IUU fishing when subsidies to expand the fishing fleet continue to be given by governments (Ho and Ngo 2023), and aquaculture is often treated separate from fishing, even though there are many connections between the two as they compete for physical space and markets (Mansfield et al. 2024). Overall, these challenges point to the need for more coordinated actions and innovative solutions, combined with hard decisions in economically lucrative sectors to find inclusive and effective ways to reduce fishing capacity, prevent mangrove conversion, and eliminate plastic pollution sources.

5 Climate Action: Adaptation and Mitigation in a Changing Climate

5.1 Introduction

The seriousness of climate change has become readily apparent in Southeast Asia, with increasingly visible impacts and risks. The region has long been subject to natural hazards, including floods, storms, heat waves, droughts, and wildfires. Countries with long coastlines and large populations in low-lying areas, such as the Philippines, regularly experience destructive typhoons, and Vietnam, with half of the Mekong Delta lying just 1 m above sea level, is at risk of immersion from sea level rise. Other countries like Laos and Cambodia have high rates of poverty that will test their ability to adapt, while potentially severe water scarcity and extreme heat are already being experienced in many urban areas. The Intergovernmental Panel on Climate Change has called for countries to pursue climate-resilient development pathways, which link mitigation, adaptation, and future economic development together, but what this will look like in practice remains unclear.

Yet if any area in the world needs such comprehensive policies, it is Southeast Asia. Greenhouse gas emissions are rising more rapidly than in nearly any other region, with high dependence on coal and petroleum, rising individual energy consumption, and slow uptake of renewables (Wang et al. 2016). Concentrations of populations and assets in coastal zones and floodplains has increased risk and reduced overall resilience as ecosystems have degraded. The combination of climate change plus the impacts of globalization have been labeled "double exposure," explaining why it is difficult to achieve resilience as economic decisions and global economic connections constrain choices available (O'Brien and Leichenko 2000). In this, Southeast Asia is a canary in the coal mine for the difficulties in moving toward climate-compatible development (Wise et al. 2016).

The SDGs, however, do not grapple with the key drivers of climate change. Most remarkably, SDG 13 does not commit countries to specific steps to tackle emissions, a glaring gap. Policies for climate in Southeast Asia have focused too much on hoped-for future financing and technology and not enough on understanding vulnerability and how current economic choices have increased it. Forest-degrading activities like logging can raise the risks of floods as well as contributing to atmosphere-warming carbon emissions, while rice production is sensitive to changes in water while also generating considerable methane emissions. Managing these risks requires an understanding that explicit considerations of climate change exposure and hard decisions about economic development strategies must be made. While there are some bottom-up initiatives emerging, they pale in comparison to the scale of the problem.

5.2 Climate Impacts and Regional Vulnerabilities

An extended spell of extreme heat in 2023 across mainland Southeast Asia saw Laos, Thailand, and Vietnam recording their highest temperatures ever. Average surface temperatures in Southeast Asia have already risen by on average 1°C since 1950, and if emissions continue at current rates, the region may experience a 3.5°C rise by the end of the century, above the global average (Shaw et al. 2022). Sea level rise has increased by a global average of 0.19 m and is likely to reach nearly half a meter at the end of the century, with higher increases possible (Zhang and Hou 2020). Even at lower levels, Indonesia will lose numerous small islands to total submersion, while low-lying deltas like the Mekong will experience consistent tidal inundation (ADB 2017). A 1 m rise would result in about 10 percent of Vietnam's population needing to be relocated (Dasgupta et al. 2009). Storms have increased in frequency and intensity in recent years as well, causing sustained economic damages and causalities: The Philippines and Myanmar are in the top twenty most affected countries from natural disasters. To call these natural disasters is, however, a misnomer, as vulnerability has increased as a result of development decisions, particularly the conversion of protective coastal ecosystems that can reduce tidal surges and prevent coastal salinity. If all of Asia's mangroves were to be lost, the number of people in the region exposed to storm surges and sea level rise would double (Blankespoor et al. 2017).

Different factors influence human vulnerability across Southeast Asia, dependent on geography, economic composition, and anthropogenic assets. Those with high dependence on agriculture face problems of erosion, flooding, and other hazards which threaten to reduce the amount of arable land available (already one of the lowest per capita of all global regions) (McElwee et al. 2023). Southeast Asia is currently the largest rice exporting region, with Thailand, Vietnam, and Indonesia the top three exporters, but projections show declines in production are likely, with effects on food security for rice importing countries, such as the Philippines. There is also likely to be more rural to urban migration in the future, including up to six million people moving out of the Mekong Delta by 2050 in high emissions scenarios, and other migration hot spots likely in central Thailand and Myanmar as water availability and crop productivity decline (Clement et al. 2021). Already, rural farmers in Cambodia who have migrated away from water-depleted areas ended up as debt-bonded labor in brick kilns, substituting one form of precarity for another (Natarajan et al. 2019). Women in particular are vulnerable to increased demands on labor and reduced access to entitlements like food as a consequence of climate change (Eastin 2018).

Currently half the population of ASEAN lives in urban areas, with Singapore, Brunei, and Malaysia most urbanized, and the rise of coastal megacities has increased risks to many. For example, Bangkok experienced devastating floods in 2011 that killed 800 people and incurred US$45 billion in economic damages, a function of both heavy rains and poor planning and governance (Marks 2015). In Indonesia, Jakarta is sinking due to its location on a wetland, land subsidence, and sea level rise, resulting in plans to relocate the capital to East Kalimantan. Many other cities face similar if less existential risks, including water shortages, housing and transport damage, and other problems. These urban vulnerabilities often affect the poor more as they are the ones likely to settle in flood-prone areas or be involved in informal work activity. Lack of public services, like domestic water access or planting of urban shade trees, compounds these problems (Marks 2019).

5.3 Drivers of GHG Emissions

Southeast Asia is a rising contributor to global GHG emissions. While overall emissions comprise less than 10 percent of the global total, Southeast Asia has some of the fastest growing rates of increase. For example, Vietnam's emissions have been rising faster than those of nearly any other country, quadrupling over the 2000–2015 period. Emissions in Southeast Asia come from one of three sources: fossil fuel use and production; land use change, which releases carbon

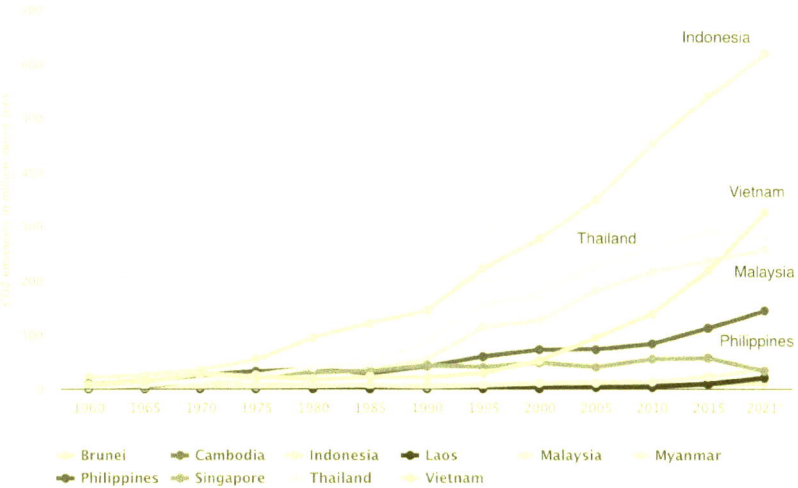

Figure 10 Territorial carbon dioxide (CO_2) emissions in Southeast Asia from 1960 to 2021, by country (*in million metric tons of CO_2*)

Source: Statista, based on data from IEA.

as forests are cleared; and agriculture, particularly methane and nitrous oxide (N_2O) from rice and livestock production. Indonesia is the single largest emitter, while in terms of per capita emissions Brunei and Singapore are highest (Figure 10) (ASEAN 2021)

Growth in energy demand has contributed to rapidly rising emissions, as has the fact that the region is highly reliant on fossil fuels, which contributed over 75 percent of energy as of 2020 (IEA 2023). CO_2 emissions from the power sector account for half of total emissions, indicating that clean electricity is the single biggest need in order to reduce carbon emissions. Indonesia, Vietnam, and Thailand are major coal producing nations, while Timor-Leste, Brunei, Myanmar, and Indonesia have important oil and gas industries, creating difficulties in moving away from dirty fuel mixes. Government subsidies for fossil fuels are valued at around $35 billion total, with the highest support in Indonesia, Malaysia, and Vietnam (ILO 2022). Only Singapore has seen overall emissions decrease in recent years despite continuing economic growth, a result of shifting from oil to natural gas for electricity generation. Renewable energy has been growing but remains only 22 percent of energy use in the region (with the exception of Laos, which generates nearly all electricity from hydropower).

Agricultural production (including from rice, livestock, and crop and land management) is an important contributor to GHG emissions for several Southeast Asian countries, accounting for 65 percent of Myanmar's emissions,

53 percent of Cambodia's, and 19 percent of Vietnam's. Rice production is responsible for 39 percent of total food system emissions in Thailand, and Asia is a major and growing source of N_2O emissions from the use of synthetic fertilizers (Panda and Yamano 2023).

CO_2 emissions from land use change are also significant, and Southeast Asia has been a regional hot spot, contributing around 15–25 percent of all global land emissions since 1980 (Calle et al. 2016). Indonesia has historically generated the highest land use emissions, primarily driven by peatland drainage and fires for cultivation of oil palm (730 Mt CO_2eq/yr, which is nearly half of the total fossil fuel emissions for the whole ASEAN region) (Panda and Yamano 2023) (see Box 2). Along with peatland and forest loss, mangroves converted to shrimp aquaculture, as noted in Section 4, also increase carbon emissions: Each pound of shrimp consumed from a deforested mangrove has an ecological footprint equivalent to 1,603 kg of emitted CO_2, far higher than beef or lamb, which are better known for being GHG-intensive (Kauffman et al. 2017).

5.4 Current Approaches to Meeting the Climate SDG Targets

SDG Target 13.1 aims at increasing resilience, while SDG 13.2 and 13.3 targets focus on integration of climate planning into everyday activities and raising education and capacity. Notably, there are no targets on mitigation (a deliberate decision that had faced country opposition). The Notre Dame Global Adaptation Initiative puts Singapore as the most prepared Southeast Asian country for climate change (ranked #7 globally) and Myanmar as the least prepared (ranked #161).[12] While the concept of "mainstreaming" climate adaptation has been advocated for decades, successes have been limited (Saito 2013). Most existing socioeconomic development plans in the region do not reflect the reality of exposure to future climate risk nor the need to reduce social vulnerabilities; rather, "initiatives to mitigate or adapt to climate change look very much like the development projects that caused climate change" (Work et al. 2019).

Lack of attention is certainly not the problem, as nearly all Southeast Asian countries have adopted national climate action plans. For example, in Thailand, a National Strategy on Climate Change Management developed in 2008 addresses vulnerability and risk issues, stressing potential damage to important economic sections like agriculture and tourism. Cambodia's plan notes the dependence of the economy on four key sectors: the garment industry, tourism, construction, and agriculture, all of which have specific risks associated with climate change. Vietnam's NDC to the Paris Agreement estimates that the cost

---

[12] https://gain.nd.edu/.

of adapting will exceed 3–5 percent of Vietnam's GDP by 2030, requiring international support and financing.

However, few of these frameworks or policies consist of comprehensive strategies to tackle both carbon emissions and climate vulnerability at the scale that is needed. Most countries have used existing institutions to tackle this new problem, with climate policies frequently coming from weaker national ministries, such as those associated with water management, like the Royal Thai irrigation department, or the MONRE in Vietnam. Of particular concern is the lack of attention by more powerful ministries, such as construction ministries responsible for building standards or planning ministries responsible for budgets (Dedicatoria and Diomampo 2018). That is, countries have looked on climate adaptation and mitigation as something to be worked out by environment ministries, not something to be dealt with synergistically across planning, economic development, and finance.

5.4.1 Adaptation Policies

Globalization has been a double-edged sword for much of Southeast Asia: It has increased wealth but at the same time decreased other elements of adaptive capacity, including access to social capital. Households across the region report more individualized production decisions and declining social relations, making people less likely to contribute to public activities (e.g., dike maintenance or sanitation programs) that would help provide resilience. Benefits from common lands (like wild-collected foods) are also on the decline due to privatization and overexploitation, leading to loss of livelihood buffers during climate events (McElwee et al. 2023).

Disappointingly, many countries have focused on only reducing physical exposures rather than addressing increasing social vulnerabilities (Box 7). Many of the projects that have been funded focus on "hard" adaptation, namely technical and infrastructure development, from urban drainage projects to deeper ports and expanded sea and river dikes. Relatively less funding has been directed toward soft adaptation measures like insurance schemes, livelihood diversification, increasing institutional capacity, or building social capital. Adaptation financing requests are often wish lists of long-standing "pet" projects from governments, which are recast as adaptation-focused (Fortier and Trang 2013). For example, in Vietnam, an enormously expensive tidal barrier at the mouth of the Saigon river, like the Thames Barrier in London, has been proposed, but would amplify flooding outside Ho Chi Minh City. Many of these hard adaptation measures often involve serious trade-offs and risk lock-in, and are often considerably more expensive than alternatives and the least likely to be pro-poor (Eriksen et al. 2021).

BOX 7 THE POLITICS OF VULNERABILITY AND ADAPTATION

Because there is no clear standard for what countries are most vulnerable to climate change, determining donor development aid for climate adaptation can become a political decision. The "Climate Vulnerable Forum" is a group of forty at-risk countries (including Vietnam, Cambodia, the Philippines, and Timor-Leste) that advocate for stronger climate action at the global level, and members have requested and received billions in adaptation funding. At the same time, there is potential danger in being seen as "too vulnerable." If a country is too hazardous or too likely to experience harm that might impact economic trajectories, then foreign direct investment (such as to build factories or expand agricultural development) might be directed to a less vulnerable place. Perceptions of higher risk can also affect sovereign credit ratings, which are the scores that countries receive, reflecting their ability to repay loans and manage finances. Moody's, which rates the fiscal strength of governments, has stated that sea level rise is likely to affect the creditworthiness of counties like Vietnam due to lost income, damage to infrastructure and other assets, or forced out-migration (Burh and Volz 2019).

For Vietnam, these politics of risk are particularly acute around the Mekong Delta. The most-dire projections of sea level rise and land subsidence (the sinking of land due to overextraction of groundwater and overbuilding of heavy structures on top of that land) mean that large areas of the Delta are likely to be subject to regular floods, if not permanent inundation, later this century. This imperils Vietnam's development planning, in which the Delta and Ho Chi Minh City (with another nine million in population) are seen as major drivers of growth.

Such thinking clearly influenced Vietnam's reactions to a report by Climate Central, a US scientific research organization, in fall 2019. The report used new methodologies to extrapolate elevation in relation to sea level and found that many areas of the world are at lower elevations than once thought and are thus even more susceptible to the impacts of sea level rise. A *New York Times* article to publicize the report used dramatic maps of high tides in the future, and declared that by 2050, "Southern Vietnam could all but disappear." The story caused great concern in Vietnam, but the response was less about the implications of increased flood risk for local populations than about the political implications. Within a day of the reporting, an "official rebuke" by the Deputy Director of Vietnam's Institute of Meteorology, Hydrology and Climate Change was issued, arguing that the Climate Central report

Box 7 (cont.)

was based on overly extreme long-term emissions scenarios and "could not be better than data provided by the Ministry of Natural Resources and Environment (MONRE)."[13] Vietnamese officials and scientists pushed their concerns that the work was "not scientific," because it projected future sea level rise by the end of the century to be around 2 m, rather than the 1 m which is deemed more likely to happen. There was also a strong feeling that Vietnamese scientists and their data should have been involved, as no data were collected on the ground in Vietnam.

Government officials particularly objected to the *New York Times*' use of the word "disappear" with regard to the Mekong Delta. Vietnamese officials stressed that they would be able to minimize the damage to the delta through land use planning, sea dikes, and other hard adaptation measures. The concerns even came to the level of then-Prime Minister Nguyen Xuan Phuc, who addressed the National Assembly and strongly affirmed "there is no scientific basis to conclude that in the next 30-50 years, the Mekong River Delta and some provinces and cities will be submerged below the level of water rise."[14] He further emphasized the Netherlands has much of its land area below sea level and still managed to be a developed and wealthy country and that Vietnam "must turn the risk from climate change ... from salt water to opportunity." To further confirm that the Vietnamese government does not believe it is at risk of losing investments in the Mekong Delta, there have been a number of publicly announced infrastructure projects to show this confidence, including major new expressways, massive irrigation works, and big urban redevelopments.

All too often, adaptation projects are not designed with and for the communities and places that are most vulnerable, and government priorities may not match those of citizens on the front line. This can result in what Sovacool (2018) has identified as enclosures (capturing resources or authority), exclusions (marginalization of people), encroachment (creation of ecological damage),

---

[13] Mai Hoang, "How Did Vietnamese Media Cover the Biggest Climate Story of the Year?" *Climate Tracker*, November 10, 2019, http://climatetracker.org/how-did-vietnamese-media-cover-the-biggest-climate-story-of-the-year/.

[14] Hoàng Thùy and Viết Tuân, "Dự Báo Đồng Bằng Sông Cửu Long Chìm Vào 2050 Là Chưa Có Cơ Sở," *VNExpress*, November 8, 2019: https://vnexpress.net/du-bao-dong-bang-song-cuu-long-chim-vao-2050-la-chua-co-co-so-4009576.html.

and entrenchment (the worsening of inequality). For example, in the Mekong Delta, proposed adaptation solutions include coastal dikes and sluice gates to guard against sea level rise, and the resettlement of households away from vulnerable areas like riverbanks (McElwee 2017). While the government views resettlement as a key adaptation option, interviews with those who moved reveal that resettlement sites often lack livelihood opportunities and have shoddily built dwellings vulnerable to storms. The sites also lack the social capital and neighborly ties of previous communities, resulting in impoverishment, social unrest, and other long-term problems, which have increased vulnerability to climate rather than reducing it (Miller et al. 2022).

5.4.2 Mitigation Policies

Although the SDGs say virtually nothing about the need for GHG emissions reductions, ASEAN countries have made pledges through their submissions to the Paris Agreement, known as nationally determined contributions (NDCs). But even if all pledges came into effect by 2030, they would only contribute to an 8 percent reduction in emissions and would not put the region on a path to net-zero emissions by 2050, as many other countries have committed to do. An estimated gap of 400 $MtCO_2e$ remains, meaning that ASEAN would have to drop emissions by an additional 11 percent by 2030 and beyond (Paltsev et al. 2018).

Interestingly, Singapore and Vietnam are the only Southeast Asian countries that have pledged to meet the goal of net-zero emissions by 2050. While Singapore has noted that they have limited potential for renewable development given scarce land area, Vietnam adopted a Renewable Energy Strategy in 2015 that led to rapid scale-out of wind and solar. At the same time, however, the country planned for seventy-seven new coal-fired power plants in the 2016–2030 National Power Development Plan, a contradictory position that both civil society and other countries objected to (Paltsev et al. 2018). This led to a rethink in the 2023 Power Development Plan, with a scaled-down dependence on coal. In 2022, Vietnam signed a Just Energy Transition Partnership (JETP) with international funders, receiving pledges of support of around $15 billion to help Vietnam peak electricity emissions in 2030 by moving to a nearly 50 percent share of renewable energy. However, the arrests of several prominent climate and energy activists in Vietnam since 2020 has raised concerns that the country is backsliding on net-zero pledges and endangering donor assistance, with speculation that energy-linked companies may be pressuring officials to scale back commitments.

Indonesia remains a particular challenge for moving to cleaner energy sources and accessing climate finance generally. While the country has pledged to reduce emissions by 29 percent from business-as-usual pathways, they are the number one coal exporter in the world. At the same time, 8 percent of the population is not connected to electricity, and low electricity prices have discouraged expansion into renewables that might increase costs to consumers (Ordonez et al. 2021). Indonesia too has signed a JETP agreement to receive $20 billion from global funders to speed up renewable deployment to 34 percent by 2030 and help Indonesia make net zero by 2050 (IEA 2023). However, a recent rapid increase in mining, particularly for nickel, has increased demand for coal for processing, which threatens the viability of the JETP, and other sources of climate financing have generally favored large-scale, low-risk projects rather than innovative or locally beneficial initiatives (Anantharajah and Setowati 2022). The commonality across both Vietnam and Indonesia has been strong governmental roles in energy supply, patronage politics and support for domestic coal industries, and concerns about higher energy prices leading to political backlash and instability (Dorband et al. 2020).

Some current policies to reduce emissions also raise questions of trade-offs and environmental justice issues. For example, the use of biofuels, like palm oil, as a substitute for fossil fuels is a driver of land use changes (Franco and Borras 2019). Hydropower is a low-carbon source of energy, but will require trade-offs in fishing, irrigation, downstream sediment deposition, or cultural benefits, and often requires resettlement to build large generating capacity. The ASEAN region currently supplies around 45 GW of energy from hydro, a substantial amount that generates electricity for millions of households, and multiple countries are planning on increased capacity, including Vietnam, Laos, Myanmar, and the Philippines. A total of 392 dams are completed, under construction or planned in the Mekong basin alone, with much of this undertaken by Chinese investment (Williams 2018), and similar developments are occurring on the Salween in Myanmar. While environmental justice protests against river exploitation are growing, with many communities pointing out their dependency on ecosystem services provided by rivers and wetlands, these dams continue to be planned and built, demonstrating the trade-offs between so-called green energy and other values like biodiversity and livelihoods.

5.5 Alternative Pathways to Address SDG 13

To solve some of these challenges, experiments in multilevel governance have combined collaborative approaches across scales and between national actors, subnational NGOs, and local communities. Cities have been a particular site of localized climate innovations, as much of the urban footprint that will exist in 2050 is yet to be built, providing an opportunity to build resilience into urban planning. Malaysia for example has been emphasizing "green cities" that integrate environment, economic competitiveness, and equity, and there have been collaborations between Thailand and Indonesia's small and mid-sized cities as sites of innovation and learning exchange (Zen et al. 2019). Transnational initiatives like the Global Covenant of Mayors for Climate and Energy have encouraged cities to come together to discuss emissions inventories, targets, climate risk assessments, and climate action plans, while the ASEAN Climate Resilience Network and 100 Resilient Cities Program are two examples of efforts that have helped promote multilevel urban governance (Fasting et al. 2021).

Approaches to community-based and locally led adaptation have also been successful in raising awareness and increasing resilience outside urban areas. For example, in Timor-Leste, the customary law institution of *tara bandu* has been mobilized to provide a framework for climate resiliency (Ensor et al. 2015), while in the Philippines climate resilience field schools help local farmers with access to information and extension services, particularly farmer to farmer exchanges (Chandra and McNamara 2018). Cost-effective "soft" measures, like storm warning systems, ecosystem-based approaches like mangrove planting, social welfare and insurance schemes, and livelihood diversification are often underfunded, despite local interest and the higher likelihood of delivering more equitable outcomes (McElwee et al. 2023). For fishing households, adaptation needs have centered on strengthening social relationships, increasing knowledge of risks, seeking alternative skills and livelihoods, and increasing access to credit (Shaffril et al. 2017).

However, where civil society is relatively weak, like in Laos, there has been less attention to these bottom-up approaches to reducing vulnerability (Lebel et al. 2018). Without local voices directly influencing decisions, authorities run the risk of inappropriate and unacceptable climate policy responses that may be counter-productive. It is also unclear the degree to which this locally led adaptation can truly turn into transformation. For example, in a case in post-typhoon Haiyan in the Philippines, even though a Tacloban Recovery and Rehabilitation Plan aimed at "resilient, vibrant, and livable" post-disaster recovery, a focus on resettlement and cash payments foreclosed other, more equitable, responses that could have avoided preexisting patronage politics (Ensor et al. 2021).

Alternatives to current fossil fuel dependence in the region will be difficult to generate. Some anti-coal activism has taken hold, with protests in the Philippines and Indonesia, often tied to health concerns from burning fossil fuels (Delina 2022; Sagbakken et al. 2021). While the Philippines is still heavily coal dependent, this activism has pushed authorities to sign onto a new coal plant moratorium and extend opportunities in distributed renewables (which can help avoid major grid disruptions during disasters) (Clark et al. 2020). Increasingly, NGOs have actively worked to ensure climate justice is embedded in policy responses (Haris et al. 2020), aiming to ensure that those who did little to contribute to rising emissions are not the ones who are asked to bear the burdens of action, and noting the need to reduce drivers of vulnerability and envision transformational pathways (McMillen et al. 2022). In Thailand, a Climate Justice Working Group has monitored impacts of market-based climate policy instruments, while other groups have promoted community-based renewable energy in Myanmar (Simpson and Smits 2018). Labor and worker-focused organizations have noted that there are many people who may lose jobs if coal and gas are transitioned out, raising attention to the concept of "just transitions."

However, political illiberalism in many countries constricts space to discuss these more sensitive economic issues (Simpson and Smits 2018), and recent chilling arrests of scholars and activists working on just transitions in Vietnam provide a warning that these topics are threatening to those who have profited off fossil fuel dependence. Civil society is also not a panacea in and of itself; while NGOs do raise awareness, provide options and data, and open discussion on key issues, critics accuse some NGOs, such as those in countries like Cambodia with restricted freedom, as "donor-dependent and artificial" (Christoplos and McGinn 2016). Partnerships with transnational advocates have provided some means of capacity building to generate more long-lasting and locally grounded solutions and actions. But more transformative climate policies and development decisions have been difficult to get on the agenda of governments in Southeast Asia.

5.6 Conclusions

Large numbers of people will continue to be vulnerable to climate change because of an unwillingness to rethink current development trajectories, but these problems are not unique to Asia. Many countries are publicly concerned about being at risk while at the same time pursuing development policies that increase their vulnerability. Southeast Asian countries are thus caught in a bind between climate change and their desired development trajectories that rely heavily on economic growth made possible by export-oriented natural resource exploitation and fossil fuel production and use. But climate change will complicate these choices: Under high-end temperature scenarios of more than 3 degrees by 2050, ASEAN countries would lose nearly 37 percent of their GDP to climate impacts (SwissRe 2021). Despite these risks, current climate planning and adaptation approaches centered on one-off projects have not changed overall development plans: Current economic growth mutes strong action on sustainability.

Yet the region faces large challenges to ensure that adaptation is transformative and addresses the underlying causes of vulnerability and risk, rather than being incremental. There are legitimate concerns that adaptation planning is just the same thing with a new label (Work et al. 2019), particularly the focus on hard adaptation at the expense of soft approaches. Similarly, strategies to reduce emissions have failed to make a dent, as GHGs continue to rise, and concerns about job losses or reduced government revenue have trumped concern over the continuing harms of air pollution, land degradation, and poor health associated with fossil fuel extraction and use. Existing climate policy planning processes have not been participatory in most countries either. Exclusionary framings of responsibility have allowed a focus on techno-managerial approaches – improving infrastructure, meeting rising energy demand with renewables – without significant changes to meet goals of climate-compatible development or transformative adaptation (Lebel et al. 2018). Yet managing the enormity of climate risk requires hard questions about how development trajectories may need to be radically reconfigured in a world that is 2 or more degrees warmer.

6 Conclusions: The Future of Sustainable Development in Southeast Asia

This Element has explored how the choices that Southeast Asian countries have made to pursue economic development have often come at the cost of environmental degradation. The region's reliance on export commodities like timber, rubber, palm oil, fish, and shrimp, as well as the expansion of industrial factories producing global consumer goods, create serious barriers to achieving sustainable development. Trade-offs that have come from overuse of ecosystems, including threats to clean air and drinking water supplies, degraded soils and polluted oceans, rising carbon emissions, and loss of species and increases in zoonotic diseases, are occurring across the region. Many countries assumed that these harms would be short-lived, replaced by better environmental quality and higher well-being as economies grew. Not only has this better environment failed to materialize, but also many people have missed out on the benefits of economic growth. Citizens suffering from air pollution or loss of lands to expropriation may not consider these development choices to have been acceptable trade-offs after all.

The SDGs have not provided a path for equitable and effective integration of economies and the environment in Southeast Asia. As a recent review of the halfway point to the SDGs noted, there is a considerable "disjuncture between the scale of transformative change needed and the current institutional and governance framework, which relies on soft and voluntary modes of steering" (Pattburg and Backstrand 2023). Countries have failed to include attention to the drivers of negative impacts in their solutions, leading to piecemeal and superficial efforts. The structure of the SDGs is also at fault, with targets oriented toward single issues, and often neither focused on culpability nor interconnected drivers. There is insufficient coordination between environmental and other goals, development processes lack inclusivity, and outcomes are not geared toward justice. Shrinking space for civil society in governance, and unclear choices about what policies work and for whom, serve as further barriers.

6.1 Current Pathways

As previous sections have shown, degradation driven by deep telecoupled ties to other regions creates friction as global capital meets local politics and livelihoods in Southeast Asia (Tsing 2005). Institutions that have caused the problem are in charge of fixing it while initiatives to bring in new voices have been limited (Eisenmenger et al. 2020). Attempts to harness these contradictions through concepts such as green growth have proven elusive as well, abstracted from current drivers of change and developed as technocratic solutions. Economic growth, excess consumption, and global trade are absent as culprits, as are the historical and structural roots of poverty, hunger, environmental destruction, and other inequities. Given that the SDGs leave out key questions regarding power and causation, it should not be a surprise that true sustainability remains inaccessible, constrained by decisions to prioritize traditional paths to economic development.

Part of the problem has been the SDGs themselves, with targets oriented toward single issues and goals at odds with one another, while technocratic and market-based solutions are often treated as panaceas. Despite aims to be integrative and indivisible, environmental issues are disconnected from other goals, with little recognition that nature and resources are also fundamental for fighting poverty or ensuring sustainable food production. Instead, they are seen as acceptable trade-offs: loss of biodiversity in return for food security, rather than a recognition that future production depends on the presence of pollinators or clean water supplied by nature. Trade-offs with other social goals like no poverty and zero hunger also loom large.

The interconnected nature of problems in Southeast Asia argues for integrated actions. Land cover change, air pollution, and zoonotic diseases can and should be tackled together through combined approaches to human well-being and the environment, rather than treated as separate problems. The food–energy–water nexus is particularly salient for the region, given pressures on forests, water supplies, and food insecurity. But this approach would require more integrated planning and facilitation of cross-sectoral approaches, moving away from siloed policies under weak ministries, and a better understanding of how to manage trade-offs (Keskinen et al. 2015). The increasing health burdens in Southeast Asia show these links extremely clearly – through rising deaths from poor air quality and heat exposure, increasing threats of HABs and zoonotic diseases, rising plastic pollution and chemical toxins from industrialized food production. These interlinked health threats present both a challenge and an opportunity for action.

The post-COVID-19 world also presents opportunities. Shorter and more localized supply chains have become more realistic; some national governments restricted exports of food in response to the crisis, and now could be an opportunity to balance food security concerns with more local production that can contribute to food sovereignty. Shortening food chains involves reducing intermediaries and focusing on better linking suppliers directly with markets, such as through farmers' markets or community-supported agriculture. Such steps have the potential to lead to improved local foodsheds that have lower environmental impacts, such as from reduced packaging and decreased food waste. Such "territorial markets" and food chains have been increasingly promoted globally (IPES-Food 2024), but not yet taken up in Southeast Asia.

6.2 Alternative Pathways

Within all these challenges there are glimmers of hope. While some scholars note that civil society-driven actions cannot always change the structural trajectories arrayed against them (Mostafanezhad et al. 2024), they can provide visions of what alternatives might look like. Attention to bottom-up inputs, rights-based claims, and local knowledge systems can lead to new policy innovations (Schleifer et al. 2022). Whether through community-based MPAs that align with traditional customs or protest movements against fossil fuels, alternative visions for sustainability and governance are being expressed throughout Southeast Asia. These countermovements have focused on creating alternatives to capital- and energy-intensive economies and community-centered foci instead of top-down environmental management. These responses have emerged in part because of continued government negligence toward root causes of problems, like pollution enforcement, that have pushed communities and citizens to act. However, other issues, such as overcapacity in fishing, are nearly impossible to tackle from bottom-up or community-focused solutions.

It is not a coincidence that alternative proposals have arisen from traditionally marginalized groups, as can be seen in the emergence of ICCAs and other actions. These local reflections have embedded stewardship through attention to motivations, capacities, and agents, lessons that can be applied elsewhere (Bennett et al. 2016). These mobilizations have often rejected market values for the environment in favor of reciprocity or other culture-driven values such as "sharing," "simplicity," "conviviality," "care," and the "commons" (Krauss 2021). Often these visions reject large-scale economic models upon which the current global order is built in favor of modes of organizing that advocate grounding in local places, whether through community agriculture or distributed renewables. There is also often a focus on resilience rather than sustainability explicitly, drawing on positive concepts of well-being rather than growth. Some of these alternative visions recognize living in harmony with nature, cultural diversity and coexistence within and between communities, in opposition to the perpetual accumulation embedded in growth. Examples include Buddhist and Islamic values that present alternative views on development which embed morality into decision-making (Rigg 2003), and which can be compared to concepts of *"buen vivir"* (living well with nature) that are now driving sustainability discussions in many Latin American countries.

A strong focus on democratic organizing, including equity for women, the poor, and Indigenous communities, alongside networking across civil society actors within the region, has also provided new opportunities for collaboration, as seen in the new ICCA Consortium, which has stressed social learning as well as advocacy. However, a major problem is that the governance structure of most Southeast Asia countries fails to provide the means to support these rights-based approaches. Sustainable environmental management has been blocked by antidemocratic forces, corruption, military rule, and continuing conflicts (particularly in Myanmar since 2021), capture by politically powerful industries, authoritarianism, and sclerotic post-socialism (Barney 2013). These political failings have led to an absence of procedural justice, as evidenced by protests against dam relocation, climate resettlement, environmental damage payouts, and other impacts, while the distributional outcomes of development remain highly inequitable.

6.3 Revisiting the SDGs

Recent work on sustainability transitions has stressed that sustainability may be an end goal, but the process to get there is just as important: "Long-term sustainability is more than meeting quantitative targets; it requires reshaping the processes of development ... Sustainable human development is not a checklist but a dynamic and continued process, and ample research, human will and political power – as well as urgency – exist to actively engage in that process" (UNDP 2020). It is not too late to foreground new visions of well-being that reflect local as well as national values in SDG processes, and the current moment presents opportunities to rethink priorities and reorient toward more inclusive and rights-based approaches, both in Asia and globally. In other regions, like Latin America, development actors in civil society are reconfiguring the SDG agenda to be more localized and "territorialized." In Brazil, for instance, nongovernmental networks have come together to propose "programs, projects or technologies aligned with the SDGs, which promote local development and the circular economy, with adaptability to other locations" as a bottom-up alternative to global indicators and targets (Galvão et al. 2024).

At the very least, new indicators could better reflect locally specific contexts and priorities than the broad and general approach of the SDGs, particularly indicators developed with more inclusive processes. Examples include "biocultural" indicators that reflect local values and ecologies, such as well-being or spiritual values (Sterling et al. 2017), while other indicators could help identify drivers and propose more integrated solutions. Even more ambitious alternatives are not impossible to imagine. Recent work on socio-bioeconomies has stressed that localized, diversified production systems that join communities together in sustainable value chains are in fact possible, and can be scaled up. For example, in the Amazon, inclusively managed forests, agricultural production focused on cooperatives, diverse production systems, value-adding, sustainable community-based fisheries, and ecotourism can support an alternative vision of development to extractive monocultures, ranching, and mining (Garrett et al. 2024). These sustainable socio-bioeconomies cannot develop, however, as long as perverse subsidies that favor large producers, unrestricted pollution emissions (especially carbon), and high consumption of unsustainable products like meat are not confronted.

Synergistic ties among communities, regions, and rural–urban linkages, rights-based approaches that foreground Indigenous values and tenure security, and safeguards for the economically vulnerable can all help realize this vision of sustainable development (Garrett et al. 2024). Similar approaches can shape discussions in Southeast Asia if future trajectories can be reframed. Rather than seeing dichotomies and oppositions like poverty/well-being, deforestation/reforestation, or fossil fuels/renewables, pathways for development could better highlight thresholds of change to build resilience and transformation (Reyers et al. 2018). In other words, it is not about applying a set of policies, instruments, and indicators to exit "underdevelopment" and reach a desired condition of "development," but a series of steps and choices that foreground well-being, local values, and resilience. Redefining well-being itself including concepts of human and ecological well-being, rather than the narrow indicators of the SDGs, is another step in the right direction (Vira 2015). These values and rights-based approaches can in turn improve equity and lead toward transformational pathways. However, as this Element has pointed out, Southeast Asia has a long way to go before that vision of an adaptive, just and sustainable future can be realized.

References

ADB (2004) *Technical Assistance (Financed by The Japan Special Fund) for the Greater Mekong Subregion Biodiversity Conservation Corridors Initiative*. Manila: Asian Development Bank.

ADB (2017) *A Region at Risk: The Human Dimensions of Climate Change in Asia and the Pacific*. Manila: Asian Development Bank.

ADB and United Nations University (2017) *Asia-Pacific Sustainable Development Goals Outlook*. Manila: Asian Development Bank.

Ahrends, A. Rachmawati, L., Sofyanto, H. and Hamilton-Hart, N. (2015) Current trends of rubber plantation expansion may threaten biodiversity and livelihoods. *Global Environmental Change* **34**, 48–58.

AIPP Badan Registrasi Wilayah Adat, Cambodian Indigenous Peoples Alliance, et al. (2022) *Reconciling Conservation and Global Biodiversity Goals with Community Land Rights in Asia*. Manila: Asia Indigenous People's Platform.

Akber, M. A., Aziz, A. A., and Lovelock, C. (2020) Major drivers of coastal aquaculture expansion in Southeast Asia. *Ocean & Coastal Management* **198**, 105364.

Anantharajah, K. and Setowati, A. (2022) Beyond promises: Realities of climate finance justice and energy transitions in Asia and the Pacific. *Energy Research & Social Science* **89**, 102550.

Andriesse, E. Saguin K., Ablo AD., et al. (2022) Aligning bottom-up initiatives and top-down policies? A comparative analysis of overfishing and coastal governance in Ghana, Tanzania, the Philippines, and Thailand. *Journal of Rural Studies* **92**, 404–414.

APEC (2014) *APEC Marine Sustainable Development Report*. Singapore: Asia-Pacific Economic Cooperation Organization.

Appelt, J. L. Rojas DCG, Verburg PH and van Vliet J (2022) Socioeconomic outcomes of agricultural land use change in Southeast Asia. *Ambio* **51**(5), 1094–1109.

Armitage, D., Marschke, M., and Van Tuyen, T. (2011) Early-stage transformation of coastal marine governance in Vietnam? *Marine Policy* **35**(5), 703–711.

Arts, K. (2017) Inclusive sustainable development: A human rights perspective. *Current Opinion in Environmental Sustainability* **24**, 58–62.

ASEAN (2017) *Fifth ASEAN State of the Environment Report*. Jakarta: ASEAN Secretariat.

ASEAN (2021) *ASEAN State of Climate Change Report: Current status and outlook of the ASEAN region Toward the ASEAN climate vision 2050*. Jakarta: ASEAN Secretariat.

Austin, K. G. Mosnier A, Pirker J, McCallum I, Fritz S and Kasibhatla PS (2017) Shifting patterns of oil palm driven deforestation in Indonesia and implications for zero-deforestation commitments. *Land Use Policy* **69**, 41–48.

Austin, K. G., Schwantes, A., Gu, Y. and Kasibhatla, P. S. (2019) What causes deforestation in Indonesia? *Environmental Research Letters* **14**(2), 024007.

Baird, I. (2014). The global land grab meta-narrative, Asian money laundering and elite capture: Reconsidering the Cambodian context. *Geopolitics* **19**, 431–453.

Barney, K. (2012) Land, livelihoods, and remittances. *Critical Asian Studies* **44**(1), 57–83.

Barney, K. (2013) *Locating "Green Neoliberalism," and Other Forms of Environmental Governance in Southeast Asia*. Kyoto: Center for Southeast Asian Studies Kyoto University.

Bennett, E. M. Solan M, Biggs R, et al. (2016) Bright spots: Seeds of a good Anthropocene. *Frontiers in Ecology and the Environment* **14**(8), 441–448.

Berdej, S. and Armitage, D. (2016) Bridging for better conservation fit in Indonesia's coastal-marine systems. *Frontiers in Marine Science* **3**, 101.

Biermann, F. Hickmann T, Sénit C-A, et al. (2022) Scientific evidence on the political impact of the Sustainable Development Goals. *Nature Sustainability* **5**(9), 795–800.

Blackmore, E. Norbury H, Mohammed E, Cavicchi SB and Wakeford R (2015) *What's the Catch? Lessons from and Prospects for the Marine Stewardship Council Certification in Developing Countries*. London: International Institute for Environment and Development.

Blankespoor, B., Dasgupta, S., and Lange, G.-M. (2017) Mangroves as a protection from storm surges in a changing climate. *Ambio* **46**(4), 478–491.

Blicharska, M. Smithers RJ, Mikusiński G., et al. (2019) Biodiversity's contributions to sustainable development. *Nature Sustainability* **2**(12), 1083–1093.

Bowen, K. J. Cradock-Henry NA, Koch F et al. (2017) Implementing the "Sustainable Development Goals": Towards addressing three key governance challenges—collective action, trade-offs, and accountability. *Current Opinion in Environmental Sustainability* **26**, 90–96.

Brandi, C. Cabani T, Hosang C, Schirmbeck S, Westermann L and Wiese H (2015) Sustainability standards for palm oil. *The Journal of Environment & Development* **24**(3), 292–314.

Breuer, A., Leininger, J., Malerba, D., and Tosun, J. (2023) Integrated policy-making: Institutional designs for implementing the sustainable development goals (SDGs). *World Development* **170**, 106317.

Bridgewater, P., Régnier, M., and García, R. C. (2015) Implementing SDG 15: Can large-scale public programs help deliver biodiversity conservation, restoration and management, while assisting human development? *Natural Resources Forum* **39**(3–4), 214–223.

Brodie, J. F. Mohd-Azlan J, Chen C, et al. (2023) Landscape-scale benefits of protected areas for tropical biodiversity. *Nature* **620**(7975), 807–812.

Brown, O., Crawford, A., and Hammill, A. (2006) *Natural Disasters and Resource Rights*. London: IIED.

Bryant, R. L. (1998) Power, knowledge and political ecology in the third world: A review. *Progress in Physical Geography* **22**(1), 79–94.

Burh, B. and Volz, U. (2019) *Climate Change and the Cost of Capital in Developing Countries*. London: UNEP and SOAS.

Büscher, B., Sullivan, S., Neves, K., Igoe, J., and Brockington, D. (2012) Towards a synthesized critique of neoliberal biodiversity conservation. *Capitalism Nature Socialism* **23**(2), 4–30.

Bush, S. and Marschke, M. (2016) Social and political ecology of fisheries and aquaculture in Southeast Asia. In *Routledge Handbook of the Environmental in Southeast Asia*, P. Hirsch, ed. 224–238. Abingdon: Routledge.

Calle, L. Canadell JG, Patra P, et al. (2016) Regional carbon fluxes from land use and land cover change in Asia, 1980–2009. *Environmental Research Letters* **11**(7), 074011.

Camacho, L. D. Gevaña DT, Sabino LL et al. (2020) Sustainable mangrove rehabilitation: Lessons and insights from community-based management in the Philippines and Myanmar. *APN Science Bulletin* **10**(1), 18–25.

Cao, Q. L. (2007) The development and sustainability of shrimp culture in Viet Nam. In *Species and System Selection for Sustainable Aquaculture*, P. S. Leung, C. -S. Lee, P. J., and O'Bryen, eds. 283–294. Ames Iowa: Blackwell.

Carlson, K. M. Curran LM, Ratnasari D., et al. (2012) Committed carbon emissions, deforestation, and community land conversion from oil palm plantation expansion in West Kalimantan, Indonesia. *Proceedings of the National Academy of Sciences of the United States of America* **109**(19), 7559–7564.

Carlson, K. M. Heilmayr R, Gibbs HK, et al. (2018) Effect of oil palm sustainability certification on deforestation and fire in Indonesia. *Proceedings of the National Academy of Sciences of the United States of America* **115**(1), 121–126.

Carr, E. (2015) Sustainable development goals offer something for everyone–and will not work. *Scientific American*. www.scientificamerican.com/article/sustainable-development-goals-offer-something-for-everyone-and-will-not-work/.

Chaigneau, T. and Daw, T. M. (2015) Individual and village-level effects on community support for Marine Protected Areas (MPAs) in the Philippines. *Marine Policy* **51**, 499–506.

Chandra, A. and McNamara, K. E. (2018) Climate-smart agriculture in Southeast Asia: Lessons from community-based adaptation programs in the Philippines and Timor-Leste. In *Resilience*, Z. Zommers and K. Alverson, eds. 165–179. Amsterdam: Elsevier

Chapsos, I. and Hamilton, S. (2019) Illegal fishing and fisheries crime as a transnational organized crime in Indonesia. *Trends in Organized Crime* **22**(3), 255–273.

Chen, S. Woodcock C, Dong L, Tarrio K, Mohammadi D and Olofsson P (2024) Review of drivers of forest degradation and deforestation in Southeast Asia. *Remote Sensing Applications: Society and Environment* **33**, 101129.

Cheng, Y. Liu H, Wang S, Cui X and Li Q (2021) Global action on SDGs: Policy review and outlook in a post-pandemic era. *Sustainability* **13**(11), 6461.

Christie, P., White, A., and Deguit, E. (2002) Starting point or solution? Community-based marine protected areas in the Philippines. *Journal of Environmental Management* **66**(4), 441–454.

Christoplos, I. and McGinn, C. (2016) Climate change adaptation from a human rights perspective: Civil society experiences in Cambodia. *Forum for Development Studies* **43**(3), 437–461.

Clark, R., Zucker, N., and Urpelainen, J. (2020) The future of coal-fired power generation in Southeast Asia. *Renewable and Sustainable Energy Reviews* **121**, 109650.

Clement, V. Rigaud KK, Sherbinin A de et al. (2021) *Groundswell Part 2: Acting on Internal Climate Migration*. Washington, DC: World Bank.

Cochard, R. Ngo DT, Waeber PO and Kull CA. 2017. Extent and causes of forest cover changes in Vietnam's provinces 1993–2013: A review and analysis of official data. *Environmental Reviews* **25**: 199–217

Colchester, M. and Chao, S. (2011) *Oil Palm Expansion in South East Asia*. Washington, DC: Rights and Resources Insitiative.

Conlu, M. T., Vera, D. B. D., and Salomon, T. (2022) *Celebrating Territories of Life in Southeast Asia*. Manila: Non-Timber Forest Products – Exchange Programme Asia.

Cros, A. Fatan NA, White A, et al. (2014) The coral triangle Atlas: An integrated online spatial database system for improving coral reef management. *PLoS ONE* **9**(6), e96332.

Curtis, P. G., Slay, C. M., Harris, N. L., Tyukavina, A., and Hansen, M. C. (2018) Classifying drivers of global forest loss. *Science* **361**(6407), 1108–1111.

Dabalà, A. Dahdouh-Guebas F, Dunn DC, et al. (2023) Priority areas to protect mangroves and maximise ecosystem services. *Nature Communications* **14**(1), 5863.

Damastuti, E. and Groot, R. D. (2017) Effectiveness of community-based mangrove management for sustainable resource use and livelihood support: A case study of four villages in Central Java, Indonesia. *Journal of Environmental Management* **203**(Pt 1), 510–521.

Damastuti, E. Groot R de, Debrot AO and Silvius MJ. (2022) Effectiveness of community-based mangrove management for biodiversity conservation: A case study from Central Java, Indonesia. *Trees, Forests and People* **7**, 100202.

Dasgupta, S. Laplante B, Meisner C, Wheeler D and Yan J (2009) The impact of sea level rise on developing countries: A comparative analysis. *Climatic Change* **93**(3–4), 379–388.

Davis, K. F., Yu, K., Rulli, M. C., Pichdara, L., and D'Odorico, P. (2015) Accelerated deforestation driven by large-scale land acquisitions in Cambodia. *Nature Geoscience* **8**(10), 772–775.

Davis, R. P. and Boyd, C. E. (2021) A comparison of the technical efficiency of Aquaculture Stewardship Council certified shrimp farms to non-certified farms. *Current Research in Environmental Sustainability* **3**, 100069.

Dedicatoria, R. M. M. and Diomampo, C. B. (2018) Status of climate change adaptation in Southeast Asia. In *Status of Climate Change Adaptation in Asia and the Pacific*, M. Alam, J. Lee, and P. Sawhney, eds. 153–182. Cham: Springer Climate.

Delina, L. (2022) Coal development and its discontents: Modes, strategies, and tactics of a localized, yet networked, anti-coal mobilisation in central Philippines. *The Extractive Industries and Society* **9**, 101043.

Derrick, B. Noranarttragoon P, Zeller D, Teh LCL and Pauly D (2017) Thailand's missing marine fisheries catch (1950–2014). *Frontiers in Marine Science* **4**, 402.

Dinh, K. V. (2019) Vietnam's fish kill remains unexamined. *Science* **365**(6451), 333.

Dislich, C., Keyel, A. C., Salecker, J., et al. A review of the ecosystem functions in oil palm plantations, using forests as a reference system. *Biological Reviews* **92**(3), 1539–1569.

Dorband, I. I., Jakob, M., and Steckel, J. C. (2020) Unraveling the political economy of coal: Insights from Vietnam. *Energy Policy* **147**, 111860.

Dressler, W. H. and Smith, W. (2023) Blood, timber and plantations: The violence of enclosing lives and livelihoods in the Philippines. *The Journal of Peasant Studies* **50**(6), 2406–2436.

Dwyer, M. (2022) *Upland Geopolitics: Postwar Laos and the Global Land Rush*. Seattle: University of Washington Press.

Eastin, J. (2018) Climate change and gender equality in developing states. *World Development* **107**, 289–305.

Ebi, K. L. Harris F, Sioen GB, et al. (2020) Transdisciplinary research priorities for human and planetary health in the context of the 2030 agenda for sustainable development. *International Journal of Environmental Research and Public Health* **17**(23), 8890.

Eisenmenger, N. Pichler M, Krenmayr N, et al. (2020) The sustainable development goals prioritize economic growth over sustainable resource use: A critical reflection on the SDGs from a socio-ecological perspective. *Sustainability Science* **15**(4), 1101–1110.

EJF (2019a) *Caught in the Net: Illegal Fishing and Child Labour in Vietnam's Fishing Fleet*. London: Environmental Justice Foundation.

EJF (2019b) *Thailand's Road to Reform: Securing a Sustainable, Legal and Ethical Fishery*. London: Environmental Justice Foundation.

Elder, M. and Ellis, G. (2023) ASEAN countries' environmental policies for the Sustainable Development Goals (SDGs). *Environment, Development and Sustainability* **25**(10), 10975–10993.

Elliott, L. (2012) ASEAN and environmental governance: Strategies of regionalism in Southeast Asia. *Global Environmental Politics* **12**(3), 38–57.

Ensor, J. Tuhkanen H, Boyland M, et al. (2021) Redistributing resilience? Deliberate transformation and political capabilities in post-Haiyan Tacloban. *World Development* **140**, 105360.

Ensor, J. E., Park, S. E., Hoddy, E. T., and Ratner, B. D. (2015) A rights-based perspective on adaptive capacity. *Global Environmental Change* **31**, 38–49.

Eriksen, S. Schipper ELF, Scoville-Simonds M, et al. (2021) Adaptation interventions and their effect on vulnerability in developing countries: Help, hindrance or irrelevance? *World Development* **141**, 105383.

Estoque, R. C. Ooba M, Avitabile V, et al. (2019) The future of Southeast Asia's forests. *Nature Communications* **10**(1), 1829.

FAO (2018) *The State of the World Fisheries and Aquaculture 2018*. Rome: Food and Agriculture Organization.

FAO (2022) *Resilience and Seizing Opportunities: Small-Scale Fisheries and Aquaculture Businesses That Thrived during the COVID-19 Pandemic in South and Southeast Asia*. Rome: Food and Agriculture Organization.

Fasting, S. et al. (2021) Climate governance and agriculture in Southeast Asia: Learning from a polycentric approach. *Frontiers in Political Science* **3**, 698431.

Ferrol-Schulte, D. Gorris P, Baitoningsih W, Adhuri DS and Ferse SCA. (2015) Coastal livelihood vulnerability to marine resource degradation: A review of the Indonesian national coastal and marine policy framework. *Marine Policy* **52**, 163–171.

Fidler, R. Y. Ahmadia GN, Amkieltiela, et al. (2022) Participation, not penalties: Community involvement and equitable governance contribute to more effective multiuse protected areas. *Science Advances* **8**(18), eabl8929.

Filho, W. L. Trevisan LV, Rampasso IS, et al. (2023) When the alarm bells ring: Why the UN sustainable development goals may not be achieved by 2030. *Journal of Cleaner Production* **407**, 137108.

Forestier, O. and Kim, R. E. (2020) Cherry-picking the sustainable development goals: Goal prioritization by national governments and implications for global governance. *Sustainable Development* **28**(5), 1269–1278.

Forsyth, T. J. (2007) Are environmental social movements socially exclusive? An historical study from Thailand. *World Development* **35**(12), 2110–2130.

Forsyth, T. (2014) Public concerns about transboundary haze: A comparison of Indonesia, Singapore, and Malaysia. *Global Environmental Change* **25**, 76–86.

Fortier, F. and Trang, T. T. T. (2013) Agricultural modernization and climate change in Vietnam's post-socialist transition. *Development and Change* **44**(1), 81–99.

Franco, J. C. and Borras, S. M. (2019) Grey areas in green grabbing: Subtle and indirect interconnections between climate change politics and land grabs and their implications for research. *Land Use Policy* **84**, 192–199.

Friess, D. A. Rogers K, Lovelock CE, et al. (2019) The state of the world's mangrove forests: Past, present, and future. *Annual Review of Environment and Resources* **44**(1), 1–27.

Friess, D. A., Thompson, B. S., Brown, B. et al. (2016) Policy challenges and approaches for the conservation of mangrove forests in Southeast Asia. *Conservation Biology* **30**(5), 933–949.

Fukuda-Parr, S. (2016) From the millennium development goals to the sustainable development goals: Shifts in purpose, concept, and politics of global goal setting for development. *Gender & Development* **24**(1), 43–52.

Gajardo, L. J. Sumeldan J, Sajorne R, et al. (2023) Cultural values of ecosystem services from coastal marine areas: Case of Taytay Bay, Palawan, Philippines. *Environmental Science & Policy* **142**, 12–20.

Galvão, T. G. Santos Lenares, RF and Martins, SL (2024). Building an ecosystem of innovative SDG-led solutions: Brazilian civil society organizations driving the 2030 Agenda implementation. In *The Quest for the Sustainable Development Goals: Living Experiences in Territorializing the 2030 Agenda in Brazil*, T. G. Galvao and H. Z. de Menezes, eds. Cham: Springer, 31–44.

Garrett, R. Ferreira, J., Abramovay, R. et al. (2024). Transformative changes are needed to support socio-bioeconomies for people and ecosystems in the Amazon. *Nature Ecology & Evolution* **8**(Aug), 1815–1825.

Gatti, R. C., Liang, J., Velichevskaya, A., and Zhou, M. (2018) Sustainable palm oil may not be so sustainable. *Science of the Total Environment* **652**, 48–51.

Gaveau, D. L. A. Pirard R, Salim MA, et al. (2017) Overlapping land claims limit the use of satellites to monitor no-deforestation commitments and no-burning compliance. *Conservation Letters* **10**(2), 257–264.

Gellers, J. C. and Jeffords, C. (2019) Environmental rights in the Asia Pacific region: Taking stock and assessing impacts. *Asia Pacific Journal of Environmental Law* **22**(2), 190–206.

Gellert, P. K. (2020) The political economy of environmental degradation and climate disaster in Southeast Asia. In *The Political Economy of Southeast Asia: Politics and Uneven Development under Hyperglobalisation*, T. Carroll, S. Hameiri, and L. Jones, eds. Cham: Palgrave McMillian Cham, 367–387.

Gerona-Daga, M. E. B. and Salmo, S. G. (2022) A systematic review of mangrove restoration studies in Southeast Asia: Challenges and opportunities for the United Nation's decade on ecosystem restoration. *Frontiers in Marine Science* **9**, 987737.

Gibbs, H. K. Ruesch AS, Achard F, et al. (2010) Tropical forests were the primary sources of new agricultural land in the 1980s and 1990s. *Proceedings of the National Academy of Sciences of the United States of America* **107**(38), 16732–16737.

Goldberg, L., Lagomasino, D., Thomas, N., and Fatoyinbo, T. (2020) Global declines in human-driven mangrove loss. *Global Change Biology* **26**, 5844–5855.

Goldman, M. (2001) Constructing an environmental state: Eco-governmentality and other transnational practices of a "green" World Bank. *Social Problems* **48**(4), 499–523.

Goss, J., Burch, D., and Rickson, R. E. (2000) Agri-food restructuring and third world transnationals: Thailand, the CP group and the global shrimp industry. *World Development* **28**(3), 513–530.

Graham, V. et al. (2016) A comparative assessment of the financial costs and carbon benefits of REDD+ strategies in Southeast Asia. *Environmental Research Letters* **11**(11), 114022.

Graham, V. Geldmann J, Adams VM, Grech A, Deinet S and Chang H-C (2021a) Management resourcing and government transparency are key drivers of biodiversity outcomes in Southeast Asian protected areas. *Biological Conservation* **253**, 108875.

Graham, V. Geldmann J, Adams VM, Negret PJ, Sinovas P and Chang H-C (2021b) Southeast Asian protected areas are effective in conserving forest cover and forest carbon stocks compared to unprotected areas. *Scientific Reports* **11**(1), 23760.

Green, S. J. White AT, Christie P, et al. (2011) Emerging marine protected area networks in the coral triangle: Lessons and way forward. *Conservation and Society* **9**(3), 173–188.

Gritten, D., Lewis, S. R., Breukink, G., Mo K, Thuy DTT and Delattre E (2019) Assessing forest governance in the countries of the greater Mekong subregion. *Forests* **10**(1), 47.

Ha, T. T. T., Bush, S. R., and Van Dijk, H. (2013) The cluster panacea?: Questioning the role of cooperative shrimp aquaculture in Vietnam. *Aquaculture* **388–391**(C), 1–10.

Ha, T. T. T., Bush, S. R., Mol, A. P. J., and Van Dijk, H. (2012a) Organic coasts? Regulatory challenges of certifying integrated shrimp–mangrove production systems in Vietnam. *Journal of Rural Studies* **28**(4), 631–639.

Ha, T. T. T., Van Dijk, H., and Bush, S. R. (2012b) Mangrove conservation or shrimp farmer's livelihood? The devolution of forest management and benefit sharing in the Mekong Delta, Vietnam. *Ocean and Coastal Management* **69**(C), 185–193.

Habibi, M. (2023) Extracting labour from the neighbour: Class dynamics of agrarian change in Sumatran oil palm. *The Journal of Peasant Studies* **50**(4), 1317–1346.

Hall, D. (2003) The international political ecology of industrial shrimp aquaculture and industrial plantation forestry in Southeast Asia. *Journal of Southeast Asian Studies* **34**(2), 125–151.

Hall, D. (2011) Land grabs, land control, and Southeast Asian crop booms. *Journal of Peasant Studies* **38**(4), 837–857.

Haris, S. M., Mustafa, F. B., and Ariffin, R. N. R. (2020) Systematic literature review of climate change governance activities of environmental nongovernmental organizations in Southeast Asia. *Environmental Management* **66**(5), 816–825.

Harkes, I. and Novaczek, I. (2002) Presence, performance, and institutional resilience of sasi, a traditional management institution in Central Maluku, Indonesia. *Ocean & Coastal Management* **45**(4–5), 237–260.

Harper, S. and Sumaila, U. R. (2019) *Distributional Impacts of Fisheries Subsidies and Their Reform: Case Studies of Senegal and Vietnam*. London: IIED.

Hasfi, N., Fisher, M. R., and Sahide, M. A. K. (2021) Overlooking the victims: Civic engagement on Twitter during Indonesia's 2019 fire and haze disaster. *International Journal of Disaster Risk Reduction* **60**, 102271.

Hatanaka, M. (2010) Certification, partnership, and morality in an organic shrimp network: Rethinking transnational alternative agrifood networks. *World Development* **38**(5), 706–716.

Heery, E. C., Hoeksema BW, Browne NK, et al. (2018) Urban coral reefs: Degradation and resilience of hard coral assemblages in coastal cities of East and Southeast Asia. *Marine Pollution Bulletin* **135**, 654–681.

Hickel, J. (2018) Is it possible to achieve a good life for all within planetary boundaries? *Third World Quarterly* **40**(1), 1–17.

Hickel, J. (2019) The contradiction of the sustainable development goals: Growth versus ecology on a finite planet. *Sustainable Development* **27**(5), 873–884.

Ho, A. N. and Ngo, P. H. (2023) Combating illegal, unreported, and unregulated fishing: A Vietnamese perspective. *The International Journal of Marine and Coastal Law* **38**(4), 681–715.

Ho, N. T. T., Ross, H., and Coutts, J. (2015) Power sharing in fisheries co-management in Tam Giang Lagoon, Vietnam. *Marine Policy* **53**(C), 171–179.

Hofman, I. and Ho, P. (2012) China's "developmental outsourcing": A critical examination of Chinese global "land grabs" discourse. *Journal of Peasant Studies* **39**(1), 1–48.

Holzhacker, R. and Agussalim, D. (2018) Introduction: Sustainable development goals in Southeast Asia and ASEAN. In *Sustainable Development Goals in Southeast Asia and ASEAN*, R. Holzhacker and D. Agussalim, eds. Leiden: Brill NV, 3–38.

Hornborg, A. (1998) Towards an ecological theory of unequal exchange: Articulating world system theory and ecological economics. *Ecological Economics* **25**, 1–10.

Hu, X. Næssa, J.S., Iordana, C.M., Huang, B., Zhaob, W., and Cherubini, F. (2021). Recent global land cover dynamics and implications for soil erosion and carbon losses from deforestation. *Anthropocene* **34**, 100291.

IEA (2023) *Navigating Indonesia's Power System Decarbonisation with the Indonesia Just Energy Transition Partnership*. Paris: International Energy Agency.

Iha, K., Poblete, P., Panda, D., and Sebastian, W. (2015) A footprint analysis of ASEAN: Ensuring sustainable development in an increasingly resource constrained world. *Asian Biotechnology and Development Review* **17**, 57–67.

ILO (2022) *A Just Energy Transition in Southeast Asia the Impacts of Coal Phase-Out on Jobs*. Geneva: International Labor Organization.

Imai, N. Furukawa T, Tsujino R, Kitamura S and Yumoto T. (2018) Factors affecting forest area change in Southeast Asia during 1980-2010. *PLoS ONE* **13**(5), e0197391-14.

IPBES (2019) *Summary for Policymakers of the Global Assessment on Biodiversity and Ecosystem Services*. Bonn: Intergovernmental Science-Policy Platform on Biodiversity and Ecosystem Services.

IPCC (2022) *Climate Change 2022 – Impacts, Adaptation and Vulnerability.* IPCC.

IPES-Food (2024) *Food from Somewhere: Building Food Security and Resilience through Territorial Markets.* Brussel: IPES-Food.

Islam, Md S, Pei, Y. H., and Mangharam, S. (2016) Trans-boundary haze pollution in Southeast Asia: Sustainability through plural environmental governance. *Sustainability* **8**(5), 499.

Ivanova, M. (2010) UNEP in global environmental governance: Design, leadership, location. *Global Environmental Politics* **10**(1), 30–59.

Jambeck, J. R. Geyer R, Wilcox C, et al. (2015) Plastic waste inputs from land into the ocean. *Science* **347**(6223), 768–771.

Kamil, K. A., Hailu, A., Rogers, A., and Pandit, R. (2017) An assessment of marine protected areas as a marine management strategy in Southeast Asia: A literature review. *Ocean & Coastal Management* **145**, 72–81.

Kauffman, J. B. Arifanti VB, Trejo HH, et al. (2017) The jumbo carbon footprint of a shrimp: Carbon losses from mangrove deforestation. *Frontiers in Ecology and the Environment* **15**(4), 183–188.

Kenney-Lazar, M. and Ishikawa, N. (2019) Mega-plantations in Southeast Asia. *Environment and Society* **10**(1), 63–82.

Kenney-Lazar, M., Suhardiman, D., and Dwyer, M. B. (2018) State spaces of resistance: Industrial tree plantations and the struggle for land in Laos. *Antipode* **50**(5), 1290–1310.

Kenney-Lazar, M., Suhardiman, D., and Hunt, G. (2023) The spatial politics of land policy reform in Myanmar and Laos. *The Journal of Peasant Studies* **50**(4), 1529–1548.

Keskinen, M., Someth, P., Salmivaara, A., and Kummu, M. (2015) Water-energy-food Nexus in a transboundary river basin: The case of Tonle Sap lake, Mekong river basin. *Water* **7**(10), 5416–5436.

Kondo, M. Sitch S, Ciais P, et al. (2022) Are land-use change emissions in Southeast Asia decreasing or increasing? *Global Biogeochemical Cycles* **36**(1), e2020GB006909.

Koplitz, S. N. et al. (2016) Public health impacts of the severe haze in Equatorial Asia in September–October 2015: Demonstration of a new framework for informing fire management strategies to reduce downwind smoke exposure. *Environmental Research Letters* **11**(9), 094023.

Koplitz, S. N. Jacob DJ, Sulprizio MP, Myllyvirta L and Reid C. (2017) Burden of disease from rising coal-fired power plant emissions in Southeast Asia. *Environmental Science & Technology* **51**(3), 1467–1476.

Kotowicz, D. M. Torell E, Castro J, Oracion EG, Pollnac R and Ricci G (2022) Exploring influences on environmental stewardship of fishing communities in fisheries management in the Philippines. *Environmental Management* **69** (6), 1102–1117.

Krauss, J. E. (2021) Decolonizing, conviviality and convivial conservation: Towards a convivial SDG 15, life on land? *Journal of Political Ecology* **28** (1), 945–967.

Kumar, C., Begeladze, S., Calmon, M., and Saint-Laurent, C. (2015) *Enhancing Food Security through Forest Landscape Restoration: Lessons from Burkina Faso, Brazil, Guatemala, Viet Nam, Ghana, Ethiopia and Philippines*. Gland, Switzerland: IUCN.

Le, T. V. H. (2021) *Competing for Land, Mangroves and Marine Resources in Coastal Vietnam*. The Netherlands: Springer.

Leach, M. Reyers B, Bai X, et al. (2018) Equity and sustainability in the Anthropocene: A social–ecological systems perspective on their intertwined futures. *Global Sustainability* **1**, e13.

Lebel, L. Käkönen M, Dany V, Lebel P, Thuon T and Voladet S. (2018) The framing and governance of climate change adaptation projects in Lao PDR and Cambodia. *International Environmental Agreements: Politics, Law and Economics* **18**(3), 429–446.

Lebreton, L. C. M., Zwet J van der, Damsteeg J-W, Slat B, Andrady A and Reisser J. (2017) River plastic emissions to the world's oceans. *Nature Communications* **8**(1), 15611.

Lee, T. M. Sigouin, A., Pinedo-Vasquez, M., and Nasi, R. (2014) *The Harvest of Wildlife for Bushmeat and Traditional Medicine in East, South and Southeast Asia: Current Knowledge Base, Challenges, Opportunities and Areas for Future Research*. CIFOR Occasional Paper.

Li, T. M. (2002) Engaging simplifications: Community-based resource management, market processes and state agendas in upland Southeast Asia. *World Development* **30**(2), 265–283.

Li, T. M. (2018) After the land grab: Infrastructural violence and the "Mafia System" in Indonesia's oil palm plantation zones. *Geoforum* **96**, 328–337.

Li, T. M. and Semedi, P. (2021) *Plantation Life: Corporate Occupation in Indonesia's Oil Palm Zone*. Durham: Duke University Press.

Liao, C. and Agrawal, A. (2024) Towards a science of "land grabbing." *Land Use Policy* **137**, 107002.

Lim, M., Jørgensen, P. S., and Wyborn, C. (2018) Reframing the sustainable development goals to achieve sustainable development in the Anthropocene—a systems approach. *Ecology and Society* **23**(3), 22.

Liu, J. Hull V, Godfray HCJ, et al. (2018) Nexus approaches to global sustainable development. *Nature Sustainability* **1**(9), 466–476.

Liverman, D. M. (2018) Geographic perspectives on development goals. *Dialogues in Human Geography* **8**(2), 168–185.

Loch, T. K. and Riechers, M. (2021) Integrating indigenous and local knowledge in management and research on coastal ecosystems in the Global South: A literature review. *Ocean & Coastal Management* **212**, 105821.

Lönngren, J. and Van Poeck, K. (2021) Wicked problems: A mapping review of the literature. *International Journal of Sustainable Development & World Ecology* **28**(6), 481–502.

Lu, Y., Yuan J, Lu X, et al. (2018) Major threats of pollution and climate change to global coastal ecosystems and enhanced management for sustainability. *Environmental Pollution* **239**, 670–680.

MacDonald, G. K., Bennett, E. M., Potter, P. A., and Ramankutty, N. (2011) Agronomic phosphorus imbalances across the world's croplands. *Proceedings of the National Academy of Sciences of the United States of America* **108**(7), 3086–3091.

Mansfield, E. J., Micheli F, Fujita R, et al. (2024) Anticipating trade-offs and promoting synergies between small-scale fisheries and aquaculture to improve social, economic, and ecological outcomes. *Npj Ocean Sustainability* **3**(1), 1.

Mao, F., Li X, Zhou G, et al. (2023) Land use and cover in subtropical East Asia and Southeast Asia from 1700 to 2018. *Global and Planetary Change* **226**, 104157.

Maraseni, T. N. Poudyal BH, Rana E, Khanal SC, Ghimire PL and Subedi BP. (2020) Mapping national REDD+ initiatives in the Asia-Pacific region. *Journal of Environmental Management* **269**, 110763.

Marks, D. (2015) The urban political ecology of the 2011 floods in Bangkok: The creation of uneven vulnerabilities. *Pacific Affairs* **88**(3), 623–651.

Marks, D. (2019) Water access and resilience to climate-induced droughts in the Thai secondary city of Khon Kaen: Unequal and unjust vulnerability. In *Urban Climate Resilience in Southeast Asia*. M. Garschagen, ed. Cham: Springer Nature, 41–62.

Marks, D., Miller, M. A., and Vassanadumrongdee, S. (2020) The geopolitical economy of Thailand's marine plastic pollution crisis. *Asia Pacific Viewpoint* **61**(2), 266–282.

Marks, D., Miller, M. A., and Vassanadumrongdee, S. (2023) Closing the loop or widening the gap? The unequal politics of Thailand's circular economy in addressing marine plastic pollution. *Journal of Cleaner Production* **391**, 136218.

Marschke, M. and Vandergeest, P. (2016) Slavery scandals: Unpacking labour challenges and policy responses within the off-shore fisheries sector. *Marine Policy* **68**, 39–46.

Masud, M. M., Kari FB, Banna H and Saifullah K. (2018) Does income inequality affect environmental sustainability? Evidence from the ASEAN-5. *Journal of the Asia Pacific Economy* **23**(2), 1–16.

Mathis, J. E., Gillet MC, Disselkoen H and Jambeck JR. (2022) Reducing ocean plastic pollution: Locally led initiatives catalyzing change in South and Southeast Asia. *Marine Policy* **143**, 105127.

McElwee, P. (2002). Lost worlds and local people: Protected areas development in Vietnam. In *Conservation and Indigenous Mobile Peoples: Displacement, Forced Settlement, and Sustainable Development*, D. Chatty and M. Colchester, eds. Oxford: Berghahn Press, 312–329.

McElwee, P. (2016a) Doing REDD+ Work in Vietnam: Will the new carbon focus bring equity to forest management? In *The Carbon Fix*. S. Paladino and S. J. Fiske, eds., Berkeley: Left Coast Press, 184–200.

McElwee, P. (2016b) *Forests are Gold: Trees, People and Environmental Rule in Vietnam*. Seattle: University of Washington Press.

McElwee, P. (2017) Vietnam's urgent task: Adapting to climate change. *Current History* **116**(791), 223–229.

McElwee, P., Huber, B., and Nguyễn, T. H. V. (2019) Hybrid outcomes of payments for ecosystem services policies in Vietnam: Between theory and practice. *Development and Change* **51**(1), 253–280.

McElwee, P. and Nghi, T. H. (2021) Assessing the social benefits of tree planting by smallholders in Vietnam: Lessons for large-scale reforestation programs. *Ecological Restoration* **39**, 52–63.

McElwee, P., Tuyến, N. P., Huệ, L. T. V., and Hương, V. T. D. (2023) Climate precarity in rural livelihoods: Agrarian transformations and smallholder vulnerability in Vietnam. *Journal of Agrarian Change* **23**(4), 661–686.

McGregor, A., Law, L., and Miller, F. (2018) *Handbook of Southeast Asian Development*. London: Routledge.

McMillan, R., Kocsis, J., and Daniere, A. (2022) Rights, justice and climate resilience: lessons from fieldwork in urban Southeast Asia. *Environment & Urbanization* **34**(1), 170–189.

Menéndez, P., Losada IJ, Beck MW, et al. (2018) Valuing the protection services of mangroves at national scale: The Philippines. *Ecosystem Services* **34**, 24–36.

Miettinen, J., Shi, C., and Liew, S. C. (2011) Deforestation rates in insular Southeast Asia between 2000 and 2010. *Global Change Biology* **17**(7), 2261–2270.

Miller, F., Ha TTP, Da HV, Thuy NTT and Ngo BH. (2022) Double displacement – Interactions between resettlement, environmental change and migration. *Geoforum* **129**, 13–27.

Milne, S. (2012) Grounding forest carbon: Property relations and avoided deforestation in Cambodia. *Human Ecology* **40**(5), 693–706.

Morand, S. and Lajaunie, C. (2021) Outbreaks of vector-borne and zoonotic diseases are associated with changes in forest cover and oil palm expansion at global scale. *Frontiers in Veterinary Science* **8**, 661063.

Morgans, C. L., Meijaard E, Santika T., et al. (2018) Evaluating the effectiveness of palm oil certification in delivering multiple sustainability objectives. *Environmental Research Letters* **13**(6), 064032.

Mostafanezhad, M., Evrard, O., and Vaddhanaphuti, C. (2024) Particulate matters: Air pollution and the political ecology of a boundary object. *Annals of the American Association of Geographers* **114**(4), 826–843.

Nam, V.N., Sasmito, S.D, Murdiyarso, D., Purbopuspito, J., and MacKenzie, R. A. (2016) Carbon stocks in artificially and naturally regenerated mangrove ecosystems in the Mekong Delta. *Wetlands Ecology and Management* **24**, 231–244.

Natarajan, N., Brickell, K., and Parsons, L. (2019) Climate change adaptation and precarity across the rural–urban divide in Cambodia: Towards a "climate precarity" approach. *Environment and Planning E: Nature and Space* **2**(4), 899–921.

Nguyen, H.-H. (2014) The relation of coastal mangrove changes and adjacent land-use: A review in Southeast Asia and Kien Giang, Vietnam. *Ocean & Coastal Management* **90**(c), 1–10.

Nguyen, L. and Keeton-Olsen, D. (2023) As livelihoods clash with development, Vietnam's Cần Giờ mangroves are at risk. *Mongabay*, February 23. https://news.mongabay.com/2023/02/as-livelihoods-clash-with-development-vietnams-can-gio-mangroves-are-at-risk/.

Nguyen, Q. and Malesky, E. (2021) Fish or steel? New evidence on the environment-economy trade-off in developing Vietnam. *World Development* **147**, 105603.

Nguyen, T. P., Tam, N. V., Quoi, L. P., and Parnell, K. E. (2016) Community perspectives on an internationally funded mangrove restoration project: Kien Giang province, Vietnam. *Ocean and Coastal Management* **119**(c), 146–154.

Norström, A., Dannenberg A, McCarney G, et al. (2014) Three necessary conditions for establishing effective sustainable development goals in the Anthropocene. *Ecology and Society* **19**(3), 8.

O'Brien, K. and Leichenko, R. M. (2000) Double exposure: Assessing the impacts of climate change within the context of economic globalization. *Global Environmental Change* **10**, 221–232.

OECD (2016) *Urban Green Growth in Dynamic Asia*. Paris: OECD Publishing.

Omeyer, L. C.M., Duncan EM, Aiemsomboon K, et al. (2022) Priorities to inform research on marine plastic pollution in Southeast Asia. *Science of the Total Environment* **841**, 156704.

Orchard, S. E., Stringer, L. C., and Quinn, C. H. (2015) Mangrove system dynamics in Southeast Asia: linking livelihoods and ecosystem services in Vietnam. *Regional Environmental Change* **16**(3), 865–879.

Ordonez, J. A., Jakob, M., Steckel, J. C., and Fünfgeld, A. (2021) Coal, power and coal-powered politics in Indonesia. *Environmental Science & Policy* **123**, 44–57.

Österblom, H., Jouffray, J.-B., Folke, C. et al. (2015) Transnational corporations as "Keystone Actors" in marine ecosystems. *PLOS ONE* **10**(5), e0127533.

Owens, K. A. and Conlon, K. (2021) Mopping up or turning off the tap? Environmental injustice and the ethics of plastic pollution. *Frontiers in Marine Science* **8**, 713385.

Paltsev, S., Mehling, M., Winchester, N., Morris, J., and Ledvina, K. (2018) *Pathways to Paris: Association of Southeast Asian Nations (ASEAN) Technology and Policy Options to Reduce GHG Emissions*. Cambridge, MA: MIT.

Panayotou, T. (1997) Demystifying the environmental Kuznets curve: Turning a black box into a policy tool. *Environment and Development Economics* **2**(4), 465–484.

Panda, A. and Yamano, T. (2023) *Asia's Transition to Net Zero Opportunities and Challenges in Agriculture*. ADB Economics Working Paper Series 694.

Pas-ong, S. and Lebel, L. (2000) Political transformation and the environment in Southeast Asia. *Environment: Science and Policy for Sustainable Development* **42**(8), 8–19.

Pattberg, P. and Backstrand, K. (2023) Enhancing the achievement of the SDGs: Lessons learned at the half-way point of the 2030 Agenda. *Int Environ Agreements* **23**, 107–114.

Paul, A., Roth, R., and Twa, S. P. S. (2023) Conservation for self-determination: Salween Peace Park as an Indigenous Karen conservation initiative. *AlterNative: An International Journal of Indigenous Peoples* **19**(2), 271–282.

Pham, T. D., Kaida N, Yoshino K, Nguyen XH, Nguyen HT and Bui DT. (2018) Willingness to pay for mangrove restoration in the context of climate change in the Cat Ba biosphere reserve, Vietnam. *Ocean and Coastal Management* **163**, 269–277.

Pham, T. T. T., Flaaten, O., Nguyen, L. T., and Vu, N. K. (2021) Subsidies—help or hurt? A study from Vietnamese fisheries. *Marine Resource Economics* **36**(4), 369–387.

Phong, N. T., Parnell, K. E., and Cottrell, A. (2017). Human activities and coastal erosion on the Kien Giang Coast, Vietnam. *Journal of Coastal Conservation* **21**, 967–979.

Phuc, T. X. and Nghi, T. H. (2014) *Rubber Expansion and Forest Protection in Vietnam*. Hanoi Vietnam: Tropenbos International and Forest Trends.

Pomeroy, R., Parks, J., Courtney, K., and Mattich, N. (2016) Improving marine fisheries management in Southeast Asia: Results of a regional fisheries stakeholder analysis. *Marine Policy* **65**, 20–29.

Pomeroy, R. S. (1995) Community-based and co-management institutions for sustainable coastal fisheries management in Southeast Asia. *Ocean & Coastal Management* **27**(3), 143–162.

Pomeroy, R. S. (2012) Managing overcapacity in small-scale fisheries in Southeast Asia. *Marine Policy* **36**(2), 520–527.

Pradhan, P., Costa, L., and Rybski, D. (2017) A systematic study of Sustainable Development Goal (SDG) interactions. *Earths Future* **5**, 1169–1179.

Prescott, J. and Steenbergen, D. J. (2017) Laying foundations for ecosystem-based fisheries management with small-scale fisheries guidelines: Lessons from Australia and Southeast Asia. In *The Small-Scale Fisheries Guidelines, Global Implementation*, S. Jentoft, R. Chuenpagdee, M. J. Barragán-Paladines, and N. Franz, eds. Cham: Springer Nature, 239–266.

Quynh, C. N. T., Schilizzi, S., Hailu, A., and Iftekhar, S. (2017) Territorial use rights for fisheries (TURFs): State of the art and the road ahead. *Marine Policy* **75**, 41–52.

Randers, J., Rockström, J., Stoknes, P.-E. et al. (2019) Achieving the 17 sustainable development goals within 9 planetary boundaries. *Global Sustainability* **2**, e24.

Reyers, B., Folke C, Moore M-L, Biggs R and Galaz V. (2018) Social-ecological systems insights for navigating the dynamics of the anthropocene. *Annual Review of Environment and Resources* **43**, 267–289.

Richards, D. R. and Friess, D. A. (2016) Rates and drivers of mangrove deforestation in Southeast Asia, 2000–2012. *Proceedings of the National Academy of Sciences* **113**(2), 344–349.

Rigg, J. (2003) *Southeast Asia, the Human Landscape of Modernization and Development*. London: Routledge.

Rigg, J. (2020) *Rural Development in Southeast Asia*. Cambridge: Cambridge University Press.

Risna, R. A., Rustini HA, Herry, Buchori D and Pribadi DO. (2022) Subak, a nature-based solutions evidence from Indonesia. *IOP Conference Series: Earth and Environmental Science* **959**(1), 012030.

Roth, R. (2004) On the colonial margins and in the global hotspot: Park–people conflicts in highland Thailand. *Asia Pacific Viewpoint* **45**(1), 13–32.

Royer, S. D., Noordwijk, M. V., and Roshetko, J. M. (2018) Does community-based forest management in Indonesia devolve social justice or social costs? *International Forestry Review* **20**(2), 167–180.

Ruysschaert, D. and Salles, D. (2014) Towards global voluntary standards: Questioning the effectiveness in attaining conservation goals The case of the Roundtable on Sustainable Palm Oil (RSPO). *Ecological Economics* **107**, 438–446.

Sachs, J. D., Lafortune, G. Fuller, G., and Drumme, E. (2023) *Implementing the SDG Stimulus: Sustainable Development Report 2023*. Dublin: Dublin University Press.

Sagbakken, H. Isataeva, A., Overland, I., Pranadi, A.D., Suryadi, B., and Vakulchuk, R. (2021). Local and global aspects of coal in the ASEAN countries. In *Handbook of Sustainable Politics and Economics of Natural Resources*, S. Tsani and I. Overland, eds. 45–63. Cheltenham: Edward Elgar.

Saito, N. (2013) Mainstreaming climate change adaptation in least developed countries in South and Southeast Asia. *Mitigation and Adaptation Strategies for Global Change* **18**(6), 825–849.

Salayo, N., Garces L, Pido M, et al. (2008) Managing excess capacity in small-scale fisheries: Perspectives from stakeholders in three Southeast Asian countries. *Marine Policy* **32**(4), 692–700.

Santika, T., Wilson KA, Law EA, et al. (2021) Impact of palm oil sustainability certification on village well-being and poverty in Indonesia. *Nature Sustainability* **4**(2), 109–119.

Sasmito, S. D., Basyuni M, Kridalaksana A, et al. (2023) Challenges and opportunities for achieving Sustainable Development Goals through restoration of Indonesia's mangroves. *Nature Ecology & Evolution* **7**(1), 62–70.

Satizábal, P., Dressler, W. H., Fabinyi, M., and Pido, M. D. (2020) Blue economy discourses and practices: Reconfiguring ocean spaces in the Philippines. *Maritime Studies* **19**(2), 207–221.

Saunders, M. I., Doropoulos C, Bayraktarov E, et al. (2020) Bright spots in coastal marine ecosystem restoration. *Current Biology* **30**(24), R1500–R1510.

Savage, J. M., Hudson, M. D., and Osborne, P. E. (2020) The challenges of establishing marine protected areas in South East Asia. In *Marine Protected Areas: Science, Policy and Management*, J. Humphries and R. Clark, eds. 343–359. Amsterdam: Elsevier.

Savage, V. R. (2006) Ecology matters: Sustainable development in Southeast Asia. *Sustainability Science* **1**(1), 37–63.

Schleifer, P., Brandi C, Verma R, Bissinger K and Fiorini M. (2022) Voluntary standards and the SDGs: Mapping public-private complementarities for sustainable development. *Earth System Governance* **14**, 100153.

Schoenberger, L., Hall, D., and Vandergeest, P. (2017) What happened when the land grab came to Southeast Asia? *Journal of Peasant Studies* **44**(4), 697–725.

Scott, J. C. (1972) The erosion of patron-client bonds and social change in rural Southeast Asia. *Journal of Asian Studies* **32**(1), 5–37.

Selgrath, J. C., Gergel, S. E., and Vincent, A. C. J. (2018) Shifting gears: Diversification, intensification, and effort increases in small-scale fisheries (1950-2010). *PLOS ONE* **13**(3), e0190232.

Sexsmith, K. and McMichael, P. (2015) Formulating the SDGs: Reproducing or reimagining state-centered development? *Globalizations* **12**(4), 581–596.

Shaffril, H. A. M., Samah, A. A., and D'Silva, J. L. (2017) Adapting towards climate change impacts: Strategies for small-scale fishermen in Malaysia. *Marine Policy* **81**, 196–201.

Shah, H. A., Huxley, P., Elmes, J., and Murray, K. A. (2019) Agricultural land-uses consistently exacerbate infectious disease risks in Southeast Asia. *Nature Communications* **10**(1), 4299.

Shaw, R., Luo, Y., Cheong, T.S., et al. (2022) Asia. In *Climate Change 2022: Impacts, Adaptation and Vulnerability.* Contribution of Working Group II to the Sixth Assessment Report of the Intergovernmental Panel on Climate Change, H. -O. Pörtner, D.C. Roberts, M. Tignor, et al., eds. Cambridge: Cambridge University Press, 1457–1579.

Simpson, A. (2018) The environment in Southeast Asia: Injustice, conflict and activism. In *Contemporary Southeast Asia: The Politics of Change, Contestation and Adaptation*, A. D. Ba and M. Beeson, eds. London: Palgrave, 164–180.

Simpson, A. and Smits, M. (2018) Transitions to energy and climate security in Southeast Asia? Civil society encounters with illiberalism in Thailand and Myanmar. *Society & Natural Resources* **31**(5), 580–598.

Sotto, L. P. A., Beusen AHW, Villanoy CL, Bouwman LF and Jacinto GS. (2015) Nutrient load estimates for Manila Bay, Philippines using population data. *Ocean Science Journal* **50**(2), 467–474.

Sovacool, B. K. (2018) Bamboo beating bandits: Conflict, inequality, and vulnerability in the political ecology of climate change adaptation in Bangladesh. *World Development* **102**, 183–194.

Srinivasan, U. T., Carey S, Hallstein E, et al. (2008) The debt of nations and the distribution of ecological impacts from human activities. *Proceedings of the National Academy of Sciences* **105**(5), 1768–1773.

Stafford-Smith, M., Griggs D, Gaffney O, et al. (2017) Integration: The key to implementing the Sustainable Development Goals. *Sustainability Science* **12** (6), 911–919.

Sterling, E. J., Filardi C, Toomey A, et al. (2017) Biocultural approaches to well-being and sustainability indicators across scales. *Nature Ecology & Evolution* **1**(12), 1798–1806.

Stibig, H.-J., Achard F, Carboni S, Raši R and Miettinen J. (2014) Change in tropical forest cover of Southeast Asia from 1990 to 2010. *Biogeosciences* **11** (2), 247–258.

Stobutzki, I. C., Silvestre, G. T., and Garces, L. R. (2006) Key issues in coastal fisheries in South and Southeast Asia, outcomes of a regional initiative. *Fisheries Research* **78**(2–3), 109–118.

Sudtongkong, C. and Webb, E. (2008) Outcomes of state- vs. community-based mangrove management in Southern Thailand. *Ecology and Society* **13**(2), 27.

Sultana, F. (2018) An(Other) geographical critique of development and SDGs. *Dialogues in Human Geography* **8**(2), 186–190.

Sumaila, U. R., Lam V, Manach FL, Swartz W and Pauly D. (2016) Global fisheries subsidies: An updated estimate. *Marine Policy* **69**, 189–193.

Suuronen, P., Pitcher CR, McConnaughey RA, Kaiser MJ, Hiddink JG and Hilborn R. (2020) A path to a sustainable trawl fishery in Southeast Asia. *Reviews in Fisheries Science & Aquaculture* **28**(4), 1–19.

SwissRe (2021) *The Economics of Climate Change: No Action Not an Option*. Zurich: SwissRe.

Tatarski, M. (2023) Tien Hai Nature Reserve latest battleground in Vietnam's push for development. *Mongabay*, September 22. https://news.mongabay.com/2023/09/tien-hai-nature-reserve-latest-battleground-in-vietnams-push-for-development/.

Taylor, M. (2013) Climate change, relational vulnerability and human security: Rethinking sustainable adaptation in agrarian environments. *Climate and Development* **5**(4), 318–327.

Teehankee, J. (2019) Accountability challenges to sustainable development goals in Southeast Asia. In Holzhacker, R. and Agussalim, D. (eds.), *Sustainable Development Goals in Southeast Asia and ASEAN*. 79–97. Leiden: Brill NV

Teh, L. C. L. and Pauly, D. (2018) Who brings in the fish? The relative contribution of small-scale and industrial fisheries to food security in Southeast Asia. *Frontiers in Marine Science* **5**, 44.

Teh, L. C. L., Teh, L. S. L., and Jumin, R. (2013) Combining human preference and biodiversity priorities for marine protected area site selection in Sabah, Malaysia. *Biological Conservation* **167**, 396–404.

Thammanu, S. Han H, Ekanayake EMBP, Jung Y and Chung J. (2021) The impact on ecosystem services and the satisfaction therewith of community forest management in Northern Thailand. *Sustainability* **13**(23), 13474.

Todd, P. A., Ong, X., and Chou, L. M. (2010) Impacts of pollution on marine life in Southeast Asia. *Biodiversity and Conservation* **19**(4), 1063–1082.

Tosun, J. and Leininger, J. (2017) Governing the interlinkages between the sustainable development goals: Approaches to attain policy integration. *Global Challenges* **1**(9), 1700036.

Tran, C. T. and Nguyen, P. Q. P. (2019) Some main causes of marine pollution in Vietnam. *European Journal of Engineering Research and Science* **4**(3), 170–175.

Tran, C. Chinh TTQ, Zhang Y and Xie Y (2020a). Economic performance of forest plantations in Vietnam: Eucalyptus, Acacia mangium, and Manglietia conifera. *Forests* **11**, 284.

Tran, D. (2024) Beyond women and men: How extractive projects perpetuate gendered violence against environmental defenders in Southeast Asia. *The Journal of Peasant Studies* **51**(1), 59–80.

Tran, N., Bailey, C., Wilson, N., and Phillips, M. (2013) Governance of global value chains in response to food safety and certification standards: The case of shrimp from Vietnam. *World Development* **45**(C), 325–336.

Tran, T. C., Ban, N. C., and Bhattacharyya, J. (2020b) A review of successes, challenges, and lessons from Indigenous protected and conserved areas. *Biological Conservation* **241**, 108271.

Triyanti, A., Bavinck M, Gupta J and Marfai MA. (2017) Social capital, interactive governance and coastal protection: The effectiveness of mangrove ecosystem-based strategies in promoting inclusive development in Demak, Indonesia. *Ocean & Coastal Management* **150**, 3–11.

Truong, T. V., Marschke M, Nguyen TV, Alonso G, Andrachuk M and Hong, PLT. (2021) Household recovery from disaster: insights from Vietnam's fish kill. *Environmental Hazards* **21**(1), 1–16.

Truong, N. V. and Chu, B. (2020) Viet Nam: Sources, impacts and management of plastic marine debris. *Environmental Policy and Law* **50**(1–2), 119–133.

Tsing A (2005) *Friction: An Ethnography of Global Connection*. Princeton: Princeton University Press.

Tsujino, R., Yumoto T, Kitamura S, Djamaluddin I and Darnaedi D (2016) History of forest loss and degradation in Indonesia. *Land Use Policy* **57**, 335–347.

Turschwell, M. P., Tulloch VJD, Sievers M, et al. (2020) Multi-scale estimation of the effects of pressures and drivers on mangrove forest loss globally. *Biological Conservation* **247**, 108637.

UNDP (2020) *Human Development Report 2020: The Next Frontier: Human Development and the Anthropocene.* New York: United Nations Development Programme.

Van, T. T., Wilson N, Thanh-Tung H, et al. (2015) Changes in mangrove vegetation area and character in a war and land use change affected region of Vietnam (Mui Ca Mau) over six decades. *Acta Oecologica* **63**, 71–81.

Vandergeest, P., Flaherty, M., and Miller, P. (1999) A political ecology of shrimp aquaculture in Thailand. *Rural Sociology* **64**(4), 573–596.

Varkkey, H. (2018) Transboundary haze, ASEAN, and the SDGs: Normative and structural considerations. In *Sustainable Development Goals in Southeast Asia and ASEAN*, Holzhacker, R. and Agussalim, D. eds., Leiden: Brill, 235–257.

Varkkey, H. (2022) Emergent geographies of chronic air pollution governance in Southeast Asia: Transboundary publics in Singapore. *Environmental Policy and Governance* **32**(4), 348–361.

Veettil, B. K., Ward RD, Quang NX, Trang NTT and Giang TH. (2019) Mangroves of Vietnam: Historical development, current state of research and future threats. *Estuarine, Coastal and Shelf Science* **218**, 212–236.

Vira, B. (2015) Taking natural limits seriously: Implications for development studies and the environment. *Development and Change* **46**(4), 762–776.

Visvanathan, C. and Anbumozhi, V. (2018) Evolutionary acts and global economic transition: Progress of the circular economy in ASEAN. In Anbumozhi, V. and Kimura, F. eds., *Industry 4.0: Empowering ASEAN for the Circular Economy*, Jakarta: ERIA, 67–105.

Vu, A. N. and Long, G. (2023) Universalism and national ownership in the context of the Sustainable Development Goals (SDGs): Perspectives from Vietnam. *International Development Planning Review* **45**(1), 41–66.

Wackernagel, M., Hanscom, L., and Lin, D. (2017) Making the sustainable development goals consistent with sustainability. *Frontiers in Energy Research* **5**, 18.

Wang, Y., Chen, L., and Kubota, J. (2016) The relationship between urbanization, energy use and carbon emissions: Evidence from a panel of Association of Southeast Asian Nations (ASEAN) countries. *Journal of Cleaner Production* **112**, 1368–1374.

Wang, Y., Hollingsworth PM, Zhai D, et al. (2023) High-resolution maps show that rubber causes substantial deforestation. *Nature* **623**, 340–346.

Warren-Thomas, E., Ahrends, A., Wang, Y., Wang, M. M. H., Jones, J.P.G. (2023) Rubber's inclusion in zero-deforestation legislation is necessary but not sufficient to reduce impacts on biodiversity. *Conservation Letters* **16**(5), e12967.

Watanabe, H. and Ubukata, F. (2023) Does international environmental certification change local production and trade practices? A case study of shrimp farming in southern Vietnam. *Human Ecology* **51**(4), 781–794.

Webb, K., Jennings, J., and Minovi, D. (2018) A community-based approach integrating conservation, livelihoods, and health care in Indonesian Borneo. *The Lancet Planetary Health* **2**, S26.

White, A. T., Aliño PM, Cros A, et al. (2014) Marine protected areas in the Coral Triangle: Progress, issues, and options. *Coastal Management* **42**(2), 87–106.

Wilcox, C., Mann V, Cannard T, Ford J, Hoshino E and Pascoe S. (2021) *A Review of Illegal, Unreported and Unregulated Fishing Issues and Progress in the Asia-Pacific Fishery Commission Region*. Hobart: FAO and CSIRO.

Williams, J. M. (2018) Stagnant rivers: Transboundary water security in South and Southeast Asia. *Water* **10**(12), 1819.

Winkler, K., Fuchs, R., Rounsevell, M., and Herold, M. (2021) Global land use changes are four times greater than previously estimated. *Nature Communications* **12**(1), 2501.

Wise, R. M., Butler JRA, Suadnya W, Puspadi K, Suharto I and Skewes TD. (2016) How climate compatible are livelihood adaptation strategies and development programs in rural Indonesia? *Climate Risk Management* **12**, 100–114.

Wolff, N. H., Zeppetello LRV, Parsons LA, (2021) The effect of deforestation and climate change on all-cause mortality and unsafe work conditions due to heat exposure in Berau, Indonesia: A modelling study. *The Lancet Planetary Health* **5**(12), e882–e892.

Wong, G. Y. Holm M, Pietarinen N, Ville A and Brockhaus M. (2022) The making of resource frontier spaces in the Congo Basin and Southeast Asia: A critical analysis of narratives, actors and drivers in the scientific literature. *World Development Perspectives* **27**, 100451.

Work, C., Rong, V., Song, D., and Scheidel, A. (2019) Maladaptation and development as usual? Investigating climate change mitigation and adaptation projects in Cambodia. *Climate Policy* **19** (Suppl.), S47–S62.

Work, C., Theilade, I. and Thuon, T. (2023) Under the canopy of development aid: Illegal logging and the shadow state. *The Journal of Peasant Studies* **50** (7), 2560–2591.

Xiao, C., Li, P., and Feng, Z. (2023) Agricultural expansion and forest retreat in Mainland Southeast Asia since the late 1980s. *Land Degradation & Development* **34**(17), 5606–5621.

Xu, Y., Yu L, Ciais P, et al. (2022) Recent expansion of oil palm plantations into carbon-rich forests. *Nature Sustainability* **5**, 1–4.

Yñiguez, A. T., Lim PT, Leaw CP, et al. (2021) Over 30 years of HABs in the Philippines and Malaysia: What have we learned? *Harmful Algae* **102**, 101776.

Yu, Y., Feng, K. and Hubacek, K. (2013) Tele-connecting local consumption to global land use. *Global Environmental Change* **23**(5), 1178–1186.

Zen, I. S., Al-Amin, A. Q., and Doberstein, B. (2019) Mainstreaming climate adaptation and mitigation policy: Towards multi-level climate governance in Melaka, Malaysia. *Urban Climate* **30**, 100501.

Zeng, Z., Estes L, Ziegler AD, et al. (2018) Highland cropland expansion and forest loss in Southeast Asia in the twenty-first century. *Nature Geoscience* **11**(8), 556–562.

Zhang, Y. and Hou, X. (2020) Characteristics of coastline changes on Southeast Asia Islands from 2000 to 2015. *Remote Sensing (Basel)* **12**, 519.

Zhang, J. J. and Savage, V. R. (2019) Southeast Asia's transboundary haze pollution: Unravelling the inconvenient truth. *Asia Pacific Viewpoint* **60**(3), 355–369.

Politics and Society in Southeast Asia

Edward Aspinall
Australian National University

Edward Aspinall is a professor of politics at the Coral Bell School of Asia-Pacific Affairs, Australian National University. A specialist of Southeast Asia, especially Indonesia, much of his research has focused on democratisation, ethnic politics and civil society in Indonesia and, most recently, clientelism across Southeast Asia.

Meredith L. Weiss
University at Albany, SUNY

Meredith L. Weiss is Professor of Political Science at the University at Albany, SUNY. Her research addresses political mobilization and contention, the politics of identity and development, and electoral politics in Southeast Asia, with particular focus on Malaysia and Singapore.

About the Series

The Elements series Politics and Society in Southeast Asia includes both country-specific and thematic studies on one of the world's most dynamic regions. Each title, written by a leading scholar of that country or theme, combines a succinct, comprehensive, up-to-date overview of debates in the scholarly literature with original analysis and a clear argument.

Cambridge Elements

Politics and Society in Southeast Asia

Elements in the Series

The Meaning of Democracy in Southeast Asia: Liberalism, Egalitarianism and Participation
Diego Fossati and Ferran Martinez i Coma

Organized Labor in Southeast Asia
Teri L. Caraway

The Philippines: From 'People Power' to Democratic Backsliding
Mark R. Thompson

Contesting Social Welfare in Southeast Asia
Andrew Rosser and John Murphy

The Politics of Cross-Border Mobility in Southeast Asia
Michele Ford

Myanmar: A Political Lexicon
Nick Cheesman

Courts and Politics in Southeast Asia
Björn Dressel

Thailand: Contestation, Polarization, and Democratic Regression
Prajak Kongkirati

Social Media and Politics in Southeast Asia
Merlyna Lim

State and Sub-State Nationalism in Southeast Asia
Jacques Bertrand

Rethinking Colonial Legacies across Southeast Asia: Through the Lens of the Japanese Wartime Empire
Diana S. Kim

Sustainable Development and the Environment in Southeast Asia
Pamela D. McElwee

A full series listing is available at: www.cambridge.org/ESEA

For EU product safety concerns, contact us at Calle de José Abascal, 56–1°, 28003 Madrid, Spain or eugpsr@cambridge.org.

www.ingramcontent.com/pod-product-compliance
Lightning Source LLC
LaVergne TN
LVHW011849060526
838200LV00054B/4255